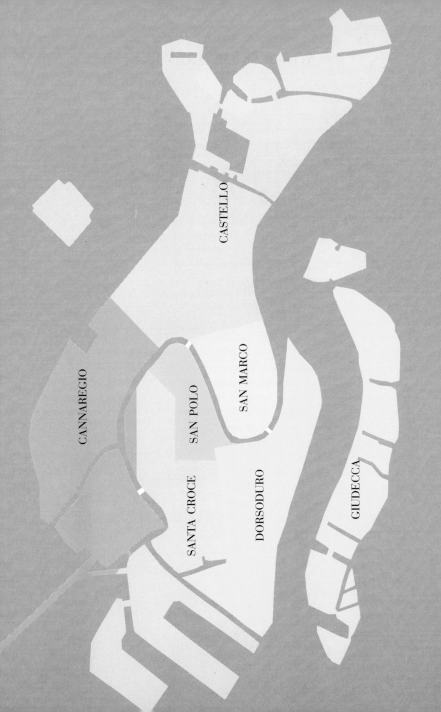

CANNAREGIO

CASTELLO

SANTA CROCE

SAN POLO

SAN MARCO

DORSODURO

GIUDECCA

ALESSANDRA BOCCATO

CHURCHES OF VENICE

ARCOBALENO

arsenale editrice

Alessandra Boccato
CHURCHES OF VENICE

photography by
Mark E. Smith

layout
Stefano Grandi

printed in Italy by
EBS Editoriale Bortolazzi-Stei
Verona

first edition
March 2001

Arsenale Editrice
A division of EBS
Via Monte Comun, 40
I - 37057 San Giovanni Lupatoto (VR)

Arsenale - EBS © 2001

ISBN 88-7743-272-1

Photography credits
99: Elio Ciol

*A special thank you
to Roberto Gondini.*
Alessandra Boccato

Maps of the islands of Murano
and Torcello have not been
included in the book.

Contents

Introduction

This book would like to accompany the reader through some of Venice's many churches. Even only a smattering of the historical and artistic facts relating to Venetian churches will, I think, help the visitor to better understand the overall evolution of the city, as well as the wealth of artistic, stylistic and architectural elements that have been "deposited" over the centuries.

I have purposefully chosen the "short chapter" format for the book, so that each church is presented in terms of its own historical chronology. The churches are also grouped according to their "sestiere", or area of the city. Obviously the descriptions of the various churches are by no means exhaustive – much will be left to the individual visitor, to his or her curiosity, senses and the emotions that the stones, paintings and precious metals will excite. My aim is simply to offer a concise, yet very precise support for the average tourist.

Venice has hundreds if not thousands of churches, and obviously not all have been included in this booklet. I have opted for those that, because of their history, their stylistic apparatus, the works of art they contain, the greats of art and architecture who have contributed to their beauty, can rightly be defined as important and interesting points in the vast and varied process of the city's development.

The reader must bear in mind that Venice was born from the waters of the lagoon, that its life depends on water, and that it could not exist as it is without this element. Water, in other words, even though it might simply seem to constitute a picturesque backdrop to the general "landscape" of the city, actually gives a specific identity to the city, and has *physical-ly* conditioned its urban development, stylistic aspect and architectural invention. Once the basic *forma urbis* was reached, everything that came afterwards had to be built respecting the confines of this lagoon body – there is, after all, no expansion beyond the watery confines of current Venice. As you will discover, there are many churches that were rebuilt in successive periods (during the Renaissance, for example), but not without re-tracing and respecting the original, perhaps Byzantine, foundations. Stylistic innovation is, in Venice, as much the result of creative judgement as necessity – and here water, that absolute limit, has imposed *verticality* where *expansion* might well have sufficed in any other context. In Italy, it is only in Venice that the bell tower, an architectural element that elsewhere juts above all other buildings and can be seen from almost all vantage points, has to vie for visibility with other architectural products such as the lay *palazzi*, houses and public buildings – and often, it is these examples of "profane" architecture that come up trumps in the visibility stakes.

Water also determines what materials can be and have been used. Transport is difficult and costly, so re-using what has already been used is almost compulsory. And this is just as common for "civic" as well as religious buildings: many churches have thus been "deconstructed" and then "reconstructed", using the older "pieces" in ways that respond much more to "modern" canons.

The booklet, however, by no means ignores what can be discovered *within* these churches. I have thus also talked about the sometimes overwhelming paintings, frescoes and statues housed in each religious building. The importance given to architects such as Codussi, Palladio and Longhena is accorded in equal quantity to the likes of Carpaccio, Titian, Tintoretto and Tiepolo, to name but a few. If the former were responsible for the "outer shell ", it is the latter who have provided the pearls within.

This book is certainly not going to unveil the treasures of Venice, and perhaps not even all of the treasures hidden in the churches covered. My hope, however, is that it might discretely accompany the visitor and help him or her to preserve the memory of those treasures.

Sestiere di San Marco

1 – St Mark's Basilica
(9th-16th centuries)

Construction began on the basilica in 829, two centuries after Torcello Cathedral. Originally a ducal chapel, it contains the body of St Mark, which the Veneti brought back from Alexandria. The building was constructed in the year 1000, and was based on Constantinople's Holy Apostles Church (since destroyed). The older mosaics can be dated to this year. The late 13th century form can be seen in one of the mosaics adorning the Door of Sant'Alipio (first on the left). At that time, the façade already had marble and mosaic decorations; the four horses, brought in 1204 from Constantinople on the fall of the Roman empire, can be found over the central doorway; the five large archways were unadorned; the large central lunette had small, Romanic arches. The building was intended to celebrate the city's economic, political and military power, and the choice of a Latin patron saint (St Mark) replacing the former, Greek patron saint (St Theodorus), underlines Venice's move away from the now powerless and decadent Byzantine empire. It must be said, however, that architecturally the basilica is very much indebted to the East. The endless decorative work culminated in the 15th century when the marble crowning section, with its vine-like leafing and pinnacles, was added. This is an example of High Gothic art (*Gotico Fiorito* in Italian). The only subsequent modifications to the basilica was the large central lunette (the small arches were replaced by a glass panel). A painting by Gentile Bellini, at the Accademia Galleries, gives a faithful view of the piazza and the basilica in this period.

The façade, much more elaborate than that of any other church, is a monument in itself. It brings together the suggestively luminous qualities of a Byzantine basilica and the narrative elements of a gothic cathedral. Five large bronze doorways (one of which now a window) lead directly to the narthex, central to Byzantine and Paleo-Christian churches. The church is laid out according to the traditional Greek cross form, with five cupolas crowned by characteristic lanterns and gold crosses. The northern façade contains important decorative elements, the remnants of former church constructions, some of which were brought back from the

East. The large, two-pilaster arch is from the St Theodorus Chapel, i.e. the original church which was later incorporated into the new construction. At the centre, superimposed over the original 13th century structure, is the *Porta dei Fiori*, a prime example of Venetian Romanic art which was given its name because of the abundance of decorative floral motifs. The lower Arab-Moorish arch is a prelude to the pointed arch. The southern façade, facing St Mark's Basin, repeats the general style of the main façade, and as it gives onto the lagoon and is right next to the Ducal Palace, it is just as ornate. The 14th century bronze door, with its small lacework arches, leads to the Baptistery. The two 6th century Syrian pilasters were originally brought to Venice as a war trophy.

Within the basilica, the glitter from the gold used in the more than 4000 square metres of mosaics is overwhelming. To ensure the faithful were familiar with sacred history, an enormous illustrated Bible was laid out over the walls. The mosaics on the southern walls, including the *Life of Christ* and *St Mark being Transported to Venice*, date to the 12th century and have been attributed to mosaicists in the Byzantine tradition; the *Passion* and *Christ Praying in the Garden*, however, are early 13th century Romanic examples, and *Genesis, The Great Flood* and the *Biblical Stories* in the atrium are attributable to the nascent Venetian school.

General galleries and the Women's Gallery (only women were allowed to use it) give onto the minor aisles. The Presbytery, built over the 9th century crypt, is aligned with the main nave and preceded by the red marble iconostasis (1394), on whose architrave we have the Delle Masegne brothers' *Twelve Apostles with the Virgin Mary and St John the Evangelist*. In the central *Ascension Vault*, we have Christ in the act of blessing, surrounded by angels and bathed in a golden light. The wealth of detail, compositional variety and chromatic splendour of the 12th century mosaic floor are outstanding. The more than 500 columns all come from different periods and deploy different materials. Of the capitals (mainly 6th-11th century Byzantine), the six golden capitals in the central nave, with their goats' heads, are unique. In the left altar there is an intriguingly primitive *Madonna with Child* (early 12th century), brought to Venice from Constantinople after the war. It was first displayed in the basilica in 1234.

The arcane, delicate light filtering in from the windows highlights the sumptuousness of the entire basilica where, according to Barbaro, "sudden bolts of lightning light our path from above, from the few lights and the mosaics of the vaults: each thing is at the same time dark and resplendent, mysterious and scintillating".

Over the centuries, artists of the calibre of Giambono, Paolo Uccello, Tintoretto, Andrea del Castagno and Palma the Younger worked on the basilica. Like any large cathedral, St Mark's is a complex world unto itself, and to appreciate its historical and artistic essence you should also visit the crypt (with its superb Veneto-Byzantine *Golden Altar-Piece*) and the loggia overlooking the Piazza.

The bell tower was given its current form in the early 16th century (it inexplicably collapsed in 1902, but was faithfully reconstructed in 1914). The tower is formed by a square, red-brick shaft topped by an arched belfry and a pyramidal steeple, and the mid-16th century *Loggetta* is by Jacopo Sansovino. He wanted to "soften" the otherwise harsh contrast between the bell tower's stark verticality and the severe horizontal line formed by the Marciana Library just behind it. The rich decorative motifs of the marble reliefs (the *Allegory of Good Government*) symbolise Venice's own idea of the perfect republic.

The Pentecost and Ascension Cupolas >

2 – Santo Stefano
14th century

Built in the 14th century over the 13th century Hermits of St Augustine complex, the church was reinterpreted in the 15th century in the High Gothic style that Venice adopted with such fervour that it quickly transformed the city's aspect. The simple façade is given a three-part structure by the pilaster strips that give form to the internal distribution. The façade is also underlined by a series of small pensile arches, and at the far ends of the architrave there are two white marble spires placed in sharp contrast with the red bricks. The rosette and large windows decorated with elegant floral reliefs frame the typically High Gothic doorway (by Bartolomeo Bon), whose pointed arch is enriched with decorative pinnacles and plant reliefs forming a crown for the figure of God.

Inside, the three aisles separated by pointed archways and columns with brightly-coloured, golden capitals lead to the polygonal apse, with its enormous gothic windows. The large presbytery above the crypt contains a 17th century main altar behind which there are the decorated, inlaid choir stalls. As in the Frari, the presbytery was originally in the middle of the nave, and was subsequently pulled down and partly rebuilt in the 16th century. The wooden ceiling closely follows the naves and is one of the most characteristic elements in the church. Its twelve-lobed section, with its delicate lines and decorations, almost seems to make the solid wooden mass of the ceiling all the lighter. The whole is covered in a rich pictorial decoration with geometrical and vine motifs, giving it a typically Venetian feel. The church houses burial monuments to some of the most famous historical characters of the city, amongst whom the most important, in the central nave, is the bronze tomb seal of Doge Francesco Morosini. The refined funeral stele for the Senator Giovanni Falier is in fact a neo-classical relief by Antonio Canova (1801). There are sculptures from the Lombardy school on all the altars, and the sacristy contains, amongst others, three paintings by Tintoretto, each from his mature period: *The Last Supper*, *The Washing of the Feet* and *Christ in the Garden*, where the artist, having reached the peak of his Baroque vision, underlines the dynamic nature of the choral, popular subjects by the use of light

and multiple perspectival points of view.

Carpaccio's *San Vitale on Horseback* (1514), originally in the nearby church of San Vidal, belongs to the artist's late maturity. Not very receptive to the revolutionary nature of Giorgione's and Titian's style, he persevered with his tried-and-tested style, where a wealth of detail coalesces to form complex narratives.

From Campo Sant'Angelo you can catch a glimpse of the leaning late Renaissance bell tower (1544).

Antonio Canova, *Funeral Stele for the Senator Giovanni Falier* (1801)

3 – San Salvador
1507-1534

The church, rebuilt in 1507 according to a project by Giorgio Spavento, in part re-used the pre-existing 12th century building, even though, according to legend, the foundations go right back to the 7th century, when Jesus reportedly appeared to St Magnus asking that a church be built there.

The façade, completed in 1663 by Giuseppe Sardi (also responsible for the nearby Scuola di San Teodoro), has a tripartite structure made up of

Titian, *The Annunciation* (1560-1565) >

two superimposed orders horizontally structured by a wide cornice and marble basement stone. The central order is crowned with a triangular tympanum with statues. The doorway, preceded by a set of steps, takes up the façade motif, adding geometrical shapes and floral wreaths.

The monumentally proportioned interior is based on the form of a cruciform basilica, with three naves with a transept and semicircular apses. The church is articulated by the double orders of pilasters which sustain the lower arches (each corresponds to one of the side chapels), and the large arches that sustain the three cupolas following the central nave. In its grandiosity, the church evokes the Marciana basilica, whose central form and the main and minor cupolas it re-elaborates, confirming the Renaissance tendency to borrow from the "ancient". When Spavento died, his work was continued by Tullio Lombardo, thus guaranteeing stylistic coherence, both architecturally and decoratively. Work was finally completed with Sansovino's classically-styled funeral monument to Doge Francesco Venier and the altar in the St Augustine chapel. Even though it was praised by contemporaries for its "modernity", the church was nonetheless very dark, and in 1567 Scamozzi thus had the three lanterns on the cupolas opened up. Now the light that fills the harmonious interior sets off the floor's magnificent marble inlays and highlights the solid elegance of the construction, lightening its severe stylistic unity. The church contains many 16th century paintings, but perhaps the most suggestive is Titian's *The Annunciation* (1560-1565), which gives us an unusual view of Venice caught in the darkening smoke emanating from a building on fire. Curiously, almost as if he wanted to underline the value of the painting, Titian signed the painting *"fecit fecit"*.

Jacopo Sansovino, *Tomb of Doge Francesco Venier* (ca. 1560) >

4 – San Giorgio Maggiore
1566-1611

Owned by the Signoria, the "Island of Cypresses", as it was once called, was the site in the 9th century of a Benedictine monastery which, in 1109, after donations from Popes and Doges, was chosen to house the remains of St Stephen the Proto-Martyr, thus giving rise to traditional Dogal processions on Christmas night.

The church complex, rebuilt in the 13th century, was restructured and extended by Palladio who planned and in part realised the refectory, the cloisters and the church, which was begun in 1566 and finished after his death. The façade, which gives onto St Mark's Basin and is a sort of counter-attraction to St Mark's Basilica, was finished in 1610 by Simone Sorella following Palladio's plans, and is based on two distinct orders reflecting the harmonious disposition of the interior. Dominated by a large pediment, it takes up the forms of a classical temple: four enormous semi-columns on a pedestal mark out a false pronaos. The two lateral wings, delimited by Corinthian pilasters and closed off by interrupted frontispieces, suggest a second, small-scale classical façade. The niches to the sides of the doorway contain statues of St George and St Stephen, both Mannerist works by Giulio Del Moro; there are portraits of Doges Memmo and Ziani in the sarcophagi above. The 18th century bell tower offers a unique view of the basin and surrounding lagoon.

The large interior, in the form of a Latin cross, lit by large windows based on those found in ancient Roman thermal baths, has three naves with an open apsidal transept under the vault – very similar, in fact, to the reception rooms of Italian villas. The main altar, isolated and placed on a slightly-raised stage, occupies the entire presbytery, beyond which there is a stately choir separated from the altar by a row of massive columns. The light plays exquisitely on the frames and capitals, confirming Palladio's characteristic love for beauty. There are two large Tintorettos on the walls surrounding the altar: *The Last Supper* and *Manna from Heaven*. The former offers an almost surreal scene, where the characters are huddled in a rustic kitchen and are surrounded by golden shafts of light which, in its concentration and dissipation, gives the idea of a vor-

tex of lights and shadows; in the latter the landscape is bathed in a strangely ominous light, and offers an intriguing backdrop to a pleasant rustic scene.

The altar in the upper chapel contains Carpaccio's *St George Killing the Dragon* (1516). This is a replica of another painting by Carpaccio, currently at the Scuola Dalmata. Here the predella is enriched with scenes from the martyrdom of the saint. Carpaccio also added scenes depicting the lapidation of St Stephen, St Jerome as a hermit, and St Benedict's repentance, thus conceptually highlighting the theme of the conflict between active and contemplative life.

Jacopo Bassano, *Adoration of the Shepherds* (ca. 1590) >

5 – San Moisè
From 1668

The church, which according to tradition goes back to the 7th century, maintained its medieval basilica form right up to its reconstruction in the 17th. The façade, a unique perspectival stage which abuts in the rectilinear form of Via XXIII Marzo, is one of the main 19th century additions to the city. It was the brainchild of Alessandro Tremignon and was completed thanks to money bequeathed by the Fini family. The heavily Baroque prospect, with scenes from the successful mercantile lives of the Fini brothers, is in the tradition of "familial aggrandising", so fashionable in the 17th century, and which alter the sacred nature of the church. The exuberant decorations and sculptural apparatus by the Flemish sculptor Meyring (Italianised to "Merengo") populate and overwhelm the geometry of the tripartite, double-ordered façade. Large Corinthian columns, ribbed and interlinked, frame the doorways crowned with the funeral portraits of various commissioners, amongst which the most striking is the bust of Vincenzo Fini on top of the so-called "eternity" obelisk. The four cardinal virtues give rhythm to the upper order, centred by a large window that is flanked by refined bas-reliefs and surmounted by two Sibyls. The family coat-of-arms over the main doorway is embedded in a series of half-tympana and underscored by a heavy, jutting cornice and is considered the crowning glory of the sumptuous decorations.

The 14th century bell tower with its fired brick spire is right next to the church.

The interior of the church, which is much less bombastic, has a groined-vaulting ceiling, and a simple nave leading to a main chapel flanked by two smaller chapels. The entire church is dominated by a main altar which has been carved out of rock, a fresco depicting Mount Sinai with God at its summit surrounded by a celestial chorus (on the chapel wall) and handing the ten commandments to the holy prophet as the people of Israel wait at the foot of the Mount. The rich 17th century art in the church is highly representative of Venetian art in the period.

6 – Santa Maria del Giglio – Zobenigo
1678-1683

The church has two names – Santa Maria del Giglio, from the lily that the
archangel gives the Virgin Mary during the Annunciation; and
"Zobenigo", from the name of the Slav family, the Jubenicos, who contributed to its foundation in the 10th century. After many restructurings,
the building was definitively rebuilt thanks to Antonio Barbaro, the
Superintendent General for the Serenissima in Dalmatia, who commissioned Sardi to make the side altars and the façade, which was intended
to celebrate the glories of the family. The commemorative scenes, which
were originally seen in Sansovino's San Zulian, strike a delicate balance
between structural design and the overwhelming superabundance of the
sculptural forms, the function of which is to amplify the composition's
upwardly-spiralling rhythm. The ostentatious façade, similar to that of
the Scalzi, has two orders with robust paired columns used to frame the
doorway, and niches containing Le Court's marble statues of members of
the Barbaro family. The curvilinear pediment surrounds the family coat-

Precious marble inlays

of-arms and brings to an end the dense profile of the surface, characterised by marked chiaroscuro effects. The statue of Barbaro as a sea captain holding a sceptre towers over the centre of the façade, almost as if to strike home all the more forcefully the church's commemorative function. The upper frames contain battle scenes underscoring the family's military prowess; there are maps of six fortified Italian and Dalmatian cities along the base (Zara, Candia, Padua, Rome, Corfu and Split). The maps, important documents in terms of the history of town planning, are a testament to Barbaro's prestigious political career. The base is the only thing left of the bell tower, which was demolished in 1775 and never rebuilt. The interior, not particularly interesting from an architectural point of view, has a single nave with side chapels and a simple presbytery framed by a triumphal arch. The marble inlays of the flooring are taken up again in the refined mosaic work on the altar-frontal of one of the altars. The church, however, contains noteworthy paintings by Rubens, Ricci, Piazzetta and Tintoretto, whose early-period *The Four Evangelists* (1552-1557) reveals a profound religious spirituality and a moving sense of human compassion. The plain ceiling contains paintings by Zanchi, whose swirling compositions offer a luminously clear chromatic scale.

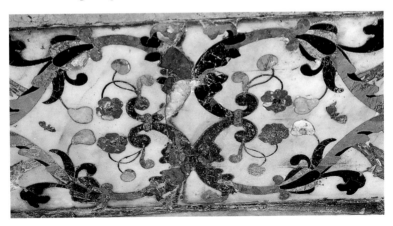

A plan of the city decorating the façade >

7

11

9

8

10

7 – San Giacometto
12th century

Even though popular tradition has it that this is the oldest church in Venice and dates construction to the 5th century, the current architectural structure actually dates back only to the 12th. Built in the heart of the market area, the 15th century clock sets the rhythm for market activities and an inscription on the outer wall of the apse urges merchants to be honest, to set their weights properly and to respect their contractual obligations.

In front of the façade there is a wooden gothic portico, dominated by a small bell-tower, built around five columns with marvellous capitals. This is one of the few examples of the gothic portico, once common to all medieval churches in Venice.

The interior of the rectangular church has three naves divided by two small spans which, along with the transept and its cupola, form a cross. The Greek marble columns, the capitals of which, holding up an 11th century pulvin, are covered in leaf motifs, originally came from much older constructions and lead the visitor's gaze down towards the three apses.

The little church was rendered all the brighter thanks to a complex chromatically vivid mosaic and paintings, which were unfortunately destroyed during the 17th century restoration (the aim was to "improve" the building while maintaining its original form). At the same time the large semicircular windows were "opened" and the altars were reconstructed. At the beginning of the 17th century, the Scuola degli Orefici e degli Argentieri (the Guild of Gold- and Silversmiths), whose famous workshops can still be admired in contemporary Venice, asked the architect Scamozzi to project an altar dedicated to St Anthony the Abbot, and Gerolamo Campagna was asked to provide the statue to the saint (now along the left nave).

Until 1542 there was a wooden pulpit in the little square in front of the church which was used for daily afternoon sermons.

8 – Santa Maria Gloriosa dei Frari
14th – 15th centuries

The Franciscan friars (or "Frari") arrived in Venice in 1222 and lived on charity. They had no permanent home until 1250, when Doge Jacopo Tiepolo gave them some land on which to build a church. This church, much smaller than the current one and facing the opposite direction, was reconstructed in the mid-14th century in the Gothic style, earning itself the nickname of "Ca' Granda" ("the big house"). The imposing brick façade, eschewing expensive materials, is in stark contrast with the sobriety of the Dominican church of San Zanipolo, built at the same time. The façade, with its huge central rosette and tripartite structure defined by pilaster strips, is adorned with small niches.

The bell tower, finished in 1396 according to a stone inscription, is one of the highest in Venice. The church's Latin cross form was given a striking transept that opens up into the presbytery, which in turn is flanked by three lateral chapels. The sacristy and the Corner chapel were added in the Renaissance. Large pillars are joined by a wooden "chain", hold up the large ogival arches and separate the three naves which are closed off by cruciform vaults. The High Gothic wooden choir was built in 1468, and is divided into three orders with 124 seats. It is contained within and delimits the large nave (decorated by Bartolomeo Bon). The church has so many Renaissance masterpieces that it is rightly felt to be one of the most import Renaissance "museums" in the city.

The *Assunta* (*Assumption*) altar-piece, concluded by Titian in 1518, towers over the main altar and dominates the entire church with its chromatic and dynamic power. The painting's emotional charge derives from the fact that the scene seems to be taking place *as* we are observing it.

The *Pesaro* altar-piece (1519-1526), an overwhelming portrait of the Pesaro family, represents Titian's break with the central representational scheme. In this painting he places the Virgin Mary's throne along a diagonal axis, and uses three distinct figurative groups to break up the work's spatial structure.

The *Madonna and Saints* altar-piece, painted by Giovanni Bellini in 1488 for the sacristy altar, is a mature work playing on the theme indi-

cated by the title. Here the figures are psychologically "humanised", placed within a devotional atmosphere where they seem to be transported by the music of the surrounding instruments and the vibrant light that fills the surrounding space.

The arrival of Donatello's wooden statue of *St John the Baptist*, originally intended for a merchants' chapel in Florence, in 1438 led to a great renewal that influenced entire generations of artists. The saint's expressive force, his disconcerting thinness accentuated by the short tunic, is one of the most realistic examples in the history of sculpture.

One of the church's main funeral monuments is *The Monument to Doge Tron* (1477-1479), Antonio Rizzo's first real masterpiece. In the work the Doge is accompanied by a series of seductive Virtues.

The *Monument to Canova*, however, an imposing Neoclassical pyramidal structure, was sculpted by Canova's students Luigi and Pietro Zandomenighi in 1827, and the small porphyry vase contains the heart of the artist, who died in 1822. The original project was Canova's, but he had intended it as a monument to Titian, who, while dying of the plague in 1576, asked to be buried in the Frari. The *Monument to Canova* was erected in front of *The Titian Mausoleum* (1835-1852).

Titian, *The Assumption* (1518) >

40

9 – San Polo
14th – 19th century

The church, founded in the 9th century and often reworked and restructured, does not have a stylistically or morphologically unitary form. However, it does have interesting architectural elements, testimony to the various transformations over the centuries. The low, elongated body of the building confers a dynamic feel to the surrounding space and occupies the vast area where bull-fights, popular dances and shooting competitions were once held. There was once a courtyard just in front of the original façade, only just visible from the adjacent Sottoportico del Caffettier; there are still two single-light mullioned windows and fragments of cornices and small pilasters from the original Byzantine building, just as there are still traces on the side nave prospect from the Gothic restructuring between the 14th and 15th centuries (pointed single-light

mullioned windows for daytime lighting, the rosette just under the bust of St Paul and the large pointed-arch doorway framed by spiralled mouldings, two *Angels Holding Scrolls* and floral motifs). The semicircular apse, with little loggias similar to those of Murano's Santa Maria and Donato, was given its current, simplified polygonal form in the 18th century.

In 1362 a bell tower was erected in front of the church. It is placed on a heavy stone base, decorated with pilaster strips and culminates in a belfry with elegant three-light mullioned windows and conic spire. The entrance door has two stone lions, one of which clasping a snake in its claws, the other a human head. According to popular tradition this is an allegorical reference to the death sentence passed on Doge Marin Faliero. The interior of the church has three naves with an apsed presbytery flanked by two chapels. The church plan is Byzantine, and has a 15th century wooden ceiling which came to light during modern restoration work. The overall structure of the church, however, was altered in 1804, when David Rossi's heavy-handed restoration radically redefined the church's identity by replacing the column along the central nave, inserting new windows and imposing an inappropriate Neoclassical decorative motif. The church nonetheless contains important works by Veronese and Palma the Younger, Tintoretto's *Last Supper* and the fourteen *Stations of the Cross* (1747-1748) by Giandomenico Tiepolo, Giambattista Tiepolo's son. Giandomenico's style is devoid of the triumphal and visionary quality typical of his father, and has a more melancholy feel, charged with meditative and almost grotesque touches. His figures, rendered with an almost striking realism, are sometimes transformed into bitter caricatures in dark chromatic tones.

Giandomenico Tiepolo, *Stations of the Cross* (1747-1748) >

10 – San Rocco
1489-1508

This church, which was built when the Venetian Republic decreed that the Scuola of San Rocco was to become a "Scuola Grande", or "Grand School", contains the remains of St Rocco, which were brought to Venice in 1485. The architect and sculptor Bartolomeo Bon was entrusted with the project for the church and he was quick to adopt Codussi's Renaissance models for his first important job. After the 1576 plague, the church became the site for celebratory rites, and the Doge was always present. Normally accompanied by the Signoria, on August 16 each year he would come to the church to give thanks to the patron saint of plague victims. A Canaletto painting shows that on these occasions the campo in front of the church would be transformed into a sort of open-air art exhi-

Canaletto, *The Doge Visiting the Church* (1735), London, National Gallery

bition, with the paintings of the best young painters hung up on the outer walls of the surrounding houses.

In order to give stylistic unity to the campo, in the 18th century Bernardino Maccaruzzi used the prospect of the Scuola itself to reconstruct the façade. The almost perfectly square surface is vertically intersected by a double order of columns with a curvilinear doorway, crowned by statues, in the middle order. The bas-relief on the doorway shows San Rocco helping the sick. Morlaiter, who had worked the bas-relief, collaborated with Marchiori on the large sculptural complex.

The interior, which was restructured in 1725 by Giovanni Scalfarotto, has conserved only the original apse chapels (the date of the original construction, 1489-1508, can still be read on the presbytery cornices). The single-nave space is punctuated by pilasters with Corinthian capitals. The pilasters, which are all grouped together and line the walls, form a frame for the side altars and the doors surmounted by circular rosettes. The refined main altar, an important example of Renaissance decorative work, holds the urn containing the body of San Rocco. The urn itself is decorated with three small frames painted by Schiavone, a 16th century painter who was one of the most sensitive interpreters of Mannerist tastes who was able to blend Venetian colour schemes and a formal academic elegance. The presbytery vault has 18th century frescoes by Giuseppe Angeli, one of Piazzetta's followers, who probably traced an original painting by Pordenone for the *Transfiguration*. The church also has one of Tintoretto's most majestic productions. His *Stories from the Old and New Testaments*, on which he worked from 1564 to 1587, is one of the maestro's religious masterpieces.

Jacopo Tintoretto's *The Flight into Egypt* (1583-1587) >

11 – San Silvestro
1837-1909

The church foundations were laid in the 9th century on a reclaimed, formerly swampy area of the city. The site chosen was in the vicinity of the Rialto markets, and the church gave onto a campo of the same name which was a hub of commercial activity and artisans' workshops (the campo has since lost its vitality in this sense). As early as the 10th century, the church was officiated by the Bishop of Grado, who lived in the nearby *fondaco*, and was the only church in the San Polo area with the function of parish church from the very outset. The building, which was originally reconstructed in the 14th century, was demolished in 1837. All that remains of the original structure is a fragment of a column with a Veneto-Byzantine capital which can still be seen in the wall facing the Rio Terrà.

The current building was designed by Santi and Meduna, and has a modest 19th century Renaissance revival façade which, having taken up preceding styles, incorporated eclectic Neogothic, Neorenaissance, Neobaroque and Neorococo elements.

The interior, which was modelled on Neoclassical schemes the elegant style of which has been extended to the altars, has a single nave with a semicircular apse and a flat ceiling. The church also contains an interesting 14th century polyptych, *The Virgin Mary, Saints and Sacred Episodes*, from the ex-Scuola dei Mercanti which was once adjacent to the church, and Tintoretto's *Baptism of Christ*.

Sestiere di Santa Croce

16

14

12

13

17

15

12 – San Zan Degolà
11th – 18th centuries

The church, erected in 1007 thanks to money donated by the Venier family, was originally built on a small island in the little group of islands of Santa Croce. The church was first restored by the Pesaro family in 1213, but this and the many subsequent restorations did not substantially modify the original Veneto-Byzantine structure that is typical of the oldest churches in Venice.

The simple, early 18th century fired brick façade reflects the interior form and structure of the church: the tripartite structure is formed by two pilaster strips which are crowned by a triangular tympanum, beneath which there is a small rosette. The head of San Giovanni Decollato, or St John the Beheaded, carved out of the brick, can be found on the right wall.

The bell tower, originally in the middle of the campo, has been annexed to the apse area of the church.

The basilica-like structure of the interior has three naves, which are separated by slim, Greek marble columns, with 11th century Byzantine capitals beneath the pointed arches. The covering, in keel-like form, is lightly decorated, and along with the fired brick floor gives a sense of warmth to the entire church (the soft, enveloping light that can be found in all Byzantine churches was designed to give a sense of intimacy and contemplation). The image of St Michael the Archangel dominates the chapel of the Holy Lord at the end of the right aisle. This splendid fresco, painted in 1300, was accidentally uncovered during the 1893 restoration. The left side chapel has a series Byzantine frescoes (13th-14th centuries), discovered in 1945.

The figures in the *Annunciation* stand out against a deep blue backdrop, while in *St Helen and Saints* St Helen's large eyes have the characteristic stare of an icon. The frescoes on the transept ceiling, showing *Christ Among the Evangelists*, surrounded by floral decorative motifs, are a rare example of 13th century Byzantine painting technique in the West.

Michael the Archangel (1300), a fresco in the Santissimo Chapel >

13 – San Giacomo dell'Orio

12th – 13th centuries

The church dates back to 1225, and a laurel tree nearby probably gave the church its name (in Italian "laurel" is *"lauro"*, whence the Venetian corruption *"orio"*). The building, despite divers styles, still maintains Veneto-Byzantine elements in the basilica-like façade and the central apse, with its small arches, pilaster strips and paterae.

The 12th century Veneto-Byzantine bell tower, a majestic square structure, is the symbol of the area's socio-economic power. The bell tower is also stylistically indebted to Torcello – two tall pilaster strips line each side of the tower, the belfry has a four-light mullioned window and the doorway has a Greek marble relief of St George (11th century).

Two basic schemes were used in the construction of the church over the years. In fact, when the church was restructured in the 14th century, the large three-nave transept was added to the original layout. We therefore have a mixture of Romanic and Gothic styles vying for prominence in the dark shadows of the church. Columns with owl-beak capitals hold up Gothic arches with grotesque 16th century decorations on wooden surface of the intrados. The green granite Ionic column was originally from Byzantium (probably from another church there). As Gabriele D'Annunzio had it: "It is like a fossil condensation from the verdure of an immense forest; following the complex ribbing, one's eye travels within the sylvan mystery". The Gothic, keel-like ceiling dominates the entire church. The wall near the entrance is made all the more interesting by a choir containing an organ, with paintings by Schiavone on the wooden shutters. Bassano, Palma the Younger, Lotto, Buonconsiglio and Veronese have provided the works for the gilded squares of the new sacristy ceiling. The magnificent Holy Sacrament chapel was added in the 16th century as a "church within the church".

14 – Santa Maria Mater Domini
1502 – 1540

Built in 960 in honour of St Christina, the church was reconstructed in the 16th century over the original Byzantine complex, most probably according to a project put together by Giovanni Buora. The Istrian stone façade, which it is thought Jacopo Sansovino completed, uses Renaissance Tuscan forms. A triangular tympanum crowns the façade and its classical volutes. There is a delicate, subtle-relief Byzantine-style bust of the Virgin Mary (16th century) over the main doorway.

The interior of the church, which is very small, has a Greek cross structure with a central Byzantine-style cupola. The local Venetian decorative language elegantly blends in with its Tuscan counterpart, and is very similar to the decorations in the church of San Giovanni Crisostomo.

The very bright church is punctuated by pilasters and stone cornices, and is enhanced by marble altars and Lorenzo Bregno's sculptures. A coloured Donatelloesque relief from the Tuscan school can be found in the apse of the main altar. *The Invention of the Cross*, with its expressive chiaroscuro, was originally painted by Tintoretto for the Scuola della Croce (built in 1561). *The Martyrdom of St Catherine* (1520), painted by Bellini's follower Vincenzo Catena, is a veritable masterpiece. A rich and seductive Veneto landscape forms the backdrop to various episodes in the life St Catherine, and Christ is highlighted and framed by a highly evocative almond-shaped shaft of light. The vaguely Nordic figures in the painting are examples of early Mannerist art.

Vincenzo Catena, *The Martyrdom of St Catherine* (1520) >

15 – Tolentini
1591 – 1602

The de Teatini congregation arrived in Venice in 1528 after the Sack of Rome, and, after trying other sites, finally set up their base in the San Nicola da Tolentino oratory.

Building began on the current complex, planned by Scamozzi, in 1591, while the façade, which was never finished, was given over to Andrea Tirali at the beginning of the 18th century. The prospect, which is different from the contemporary and highly theatrical façades of the Scalzi and Gesuiti churches, is a very cultured reworking of classical forms. A large stair-case introduces a hexastyle pronaos which is closed off by the pediment and its single, oval-shaped window. The Greek-Roman temple form, its sober decorations and the use of white Istrian stone, were a foretaste of the Venetian Neoclassical style.

The interior, so obviously based on Palladian forms, is a Latin cross with a single, wide nave. The three side chapels are separated by wall septa and are framed by decorated arches. Corinthian pilasters line the walls, with Roman windows providing abundant light for the entire church. Over the transept we can still see the tambour of the cupola, which was replaced in the 18th century by a plain, frescoed ceiling.

The 18th century main altar, behind which there is a large rectangular choir, is by Longhena with sculptures by Le Court. The opulent funeral monument to the Venetian Patriarch Francesco Morosini (lining a wall of the presbytery) is a Bernini-esque Baroque masterpiece by Parodi.

The richly-adorned church also contains paintings by Palma the Younger, Padovanino, De Pitati and Liss (whose *Vision of St Jerome* [1628] mixes a brightly-coloured, misty atmosphere and a light Baroque touch in rep-resenting the central scene). The *St Lawrence asking for Alms* (1640), with its highly-charged, densely brush-stroked realism, is a masterpieces by Strozzi, who helped transform Venetian painting towards freer and more original forms.

16 – San Stae
1678 – 1710

The medieval church was built in 1678 based on a project by Giovanni Grassi, who also changed the church's orientation so that it faced the Grand Canal.

In 1709, thanks to money bequeathed by Alvise II Mocenigo (buried in the church), a contest was held for the prospect. Rossi's was chosen over the other eleven presented – his, after all, was the closest to the 18th century Neoclassical and Neo-Palladian style, and therefore about as different as possible to Romanic and Baroque excess.

The façade that theatrically frames the landscape has a single order, and the two tight side wings correspond to the chapels inside the church. Four large Corinthian semi-columns, placed on a very high base, give rhythm to the surface and hold up the triangular tympanum crowned with statues and containing a marble rosette. The doorway, framed by niches and bas-reliefs, is topped off with an interrupted tympanum with a group of statues.

The rather conventional interior has a single wide rectangular nave with a vaulted ceiling, side chapels and a slightly raised presbytery. The light floods in from the large windows, and there are paintings in the presbytery by some of Venice's most famous 18th century painters – Ricci (who frescoed the ceiling), Pittoni, Piazzetta and Tiepolo. There are twelve paintings of the apostles, but of these Piazzetta's *Martyrdom of St James* is perhaps the most interesting. In this painting Piazzetta, abandoning his sombre chiaroscuro technique, reinvents the "transparent" quality of the colours, used to give warmth and a special plastic quality to the subjects. Tiepolo's early *Martyrdom of St Bartholomew* is still obviously in the Baroque style, but he is already delicately playing with the dialectics of colour – penetrating whites, forceful reds and electrifying blues are craftily used to give the composition its great force.

17 – San Simeon Piccolo
1718 – 1738

This currently deconsecrated church is called San Simeon Piccolo to distinguish it from the nearby San Simeon Grande, and it maintained the name despite the exhaustive 18th century reconstruction undertaken by Giovanni Scalfarotto.

The monumental building, whose image is reflected in the waters of the Grand Canal, offers extremely interesting solutions both in terms of complexity and architectural and artistic citations. It is a unique blend of different architectural motifs – from the circular structure that is a sort of re-reading of the classical Pantheon form, to the high brass-covered oval cupola (echoing Veneto-Byzantine forms), which almost seems to be competing with the dome of the Salute. The Neopalladian façade, which, like the Tolentini, has been reinterpreted and placed on a very high base, recalls the front of a Greek temple. From the majestic flight of steps the visitor is led to the Corinthian pronaos which is finished off with a triangular tympanum. The tympanum has been decorated, according to classical style, with a marble relief of the church's titular saints.

The interior, given its own special "rhythm" by the columns and pilaster strips, has a circular form with two projecting lateral wings with niches and covered by the very high cupola with lantern. Along the walls there are the four symmetrical altars, surmounted by rectangular windows, and the exedra presbytery, which has its own little cupola and is flanked by a small bell tower.

The church's subterranean complex, which is a burial area occupying the basement of the building, is unique and unusual. There is a single, octagonal room which leads to the burial rooms via four corridors whose walls are frescoed with devotional scenes, images of death and the Day of Judgement.

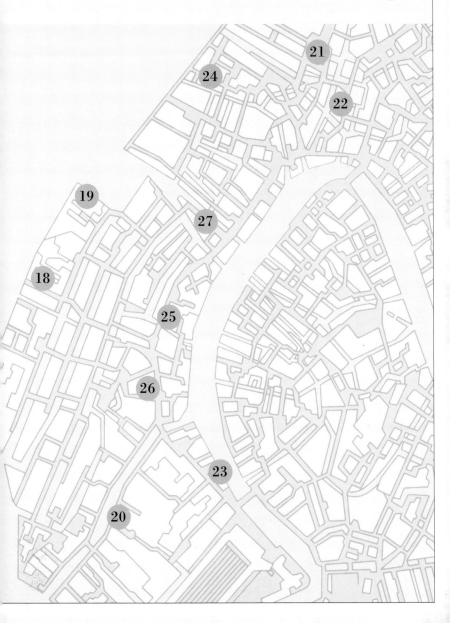

18 – Sant'Alvise
14th century

This suggestive little church, with its late 14th century Gothic convent form, was built in one of the most solitary yet popular sites in Venice. It was originally commissioned by the noblewoman Antonia Venier in 1383, when St Louis d'Anjou ("Sant'Alvise" in Venetian) appeared to her in a dream.

The sloping brick façade, with its six pilaster strips, is crowned with a series of pointed arches. The doorway is particularly interesting because of the prothyrum, a canopy-like structure held up by two scrolled columns and a series of spires, in the centre of which there is a statue of Sant'Alvise by Agostino di Duccio (15th century).

The interior, with a single nave, was completely modified in the 17th century, with the addition of the side altars and the plain frescoed ceiling (Pietro Ricchi and Antonio Torri are the authors of the bold Baroque perspectival architectural representations of the ceiling). There are still traces of the original Gothic structure in the apse, while, above the entrance, we have one of Venice's first pensile choirs (which was reserved for the nuns from the nearby convent), held up by exquisitely carved Gothic columns and beams. The floor is paved with Renaissance burial stones.

Besides Lazzaro Bastiani's 15th century altar-step, containing nine small tables depicting Biblical stories, there are three extremely important and theatrically dramatic religious works by Tiepolo: *The Crowning with Thorns*, *The Flagellation* and *The Ascent to Calvary* (all circa 1740).

The 14th century brickwork bell tower, with cone-shaped spire and four small belfries, can be found behind the church.

19 – Madonna dell'Orto
14th – 15th centuries

The church was originally built in the 14th century in honour of St Christopher, and was later called "Madonna dell'Orto" because of a *Madonna and Child* that was popularly thought to have miraculous, healing properties. The *Madonna and Child* was sculpted by Giovanni de Santi, and had originally been placed in the garden (or *"orto"*), whence it had to be moved because of the enormous numbers of pilgrims. It was then placed in the church, and it is currently in the St Mark's chapel along the left aisle.

The red brick façade, with its three-part structure punctuated by large pilaster strips (based on San Zanipolo and the Frari), has a very distinctive array of niches along the sloping sides of the façade. This disposition was originally used in Romanic churches, and Madonna dell'Orto is now the only remaining example in Venice. The niches now contain twelve statues of the Apostles by the Delle Masegne brothers. The aediculae under the spires now house 18th century statues of *Faith* and the *Cardinal Virtues*, moved to the church in 1845 with the restoration work promoted by the then Austrian government. The doorway, with a statue of St Christopher between the Virgin Mary and the Archangel Gabriel, was designed in 1460 by the architect Bartolomeo Bon (also responsible for the Porta della Carta in the Ducal Palace), and clearly belongs to a transitional phase between the Gothic (the highly-flourished external arch) and the Renaissance (the semicircular arch found inside). The coats-of-arms on either side of the doorway belong to the family of Fra' Marco Tiberio de' Tiberi, the church founder.

The 15th century bell tower, with a cone-shaped brick Renaissance cupola, is topped by a statue of the Redeemer, with the four Evangelists positioned along the sides of the belfry. All the statues are from the Lombardo school.

The herring-bone stone pavement in front of the church is one of the few examples still extant in Venice of what was a traditional technique.

The interior of the church has three naves separated by Greek marble columns with identical capitals. There is no transept, but there is a cen-

tral pentagonal apse, small side apses and a simple wooden truss covering. The clarity and simplicity of the interior, combined with the light from the large rosette and windows on the façade as well as the openings along the walls of the central nave communicate a profound sense of balance and equilibrium.

Along the left aisle, framed by a triumphal arch, there is the sober Valier Chapel (1526), an interesting example of Renaissance architecture based on a project by Andrea Buora. The church also contains a terse, Renaissance altar-piece depicting St John the Baptist and other saints (1493) by Cima da Conegliano. If you look closely, you can actually see the Castle of Conegliano and the Basilica of St Anthony (Padua) among the hills forming the backdrop.

Tintoretto is buried in the presbytery chapel, on the right. While still young, Tintoretto painted quite a few works for the church, amongst which his very theatrical *Day of Judgement*, *The Golden Calf* and *The Presentation of the Virgin Mary in the Temple* for the outer doors of the old organ. This scene, later taken up by Titian (albeit in much more realistic terms), contains imposing Michelangelo-like figures immersed in violently contrasting rays of light in a giddying perspectival composition. According to Tiepolo's biographers, the artist used a small theatre, within which he suspended his figures and, using lighted torches, then closely studied the lighting and general composition for his paintings.

The church also originally housed Giovanni Bellini's *Madonna with Child*, which was unfortunately stolen a few years ago and has never been recovered.

Cima da Conegliano, *St John the Baptist Surrounded by Saints* (1493-1495) >

20 – San Giobbe
1450 – 1493

There is very little trace of the original late-Gothic church begun by Antonio Gambello in 1450 – the brick bell tower with double-light mullioned windows in Istrian stone, the three sharply-arched windows on the southern façade, the ante-sacristy and the remaining wing of the cloister, with the portico and the so-called "capital room". In 1470, Lombardo was called on to continue the building. Lombardo provided one of the earliest examples of Renaissance architecture in Venice, as can be seen in the constructive and decorative elegance of the doorway which, with its curvilinear frontispiece based on Florentine models, opens up on a three-lobed façade very similar to San Giovanni in Bragora.

The interior, with a single nave (originally covered by wooden trusses), has a series of chapels along the left wall, the most interesting of which is the Martini Chapel. Built by a rich merchant family from Lucca, the chapel is introduced by an arch decorated with fruit and leaf motifs, and the vault has a series of polychrome terracotta decorations from the Robbian school. Here, in a completely autonomous part of the church, we can see how the Tuscan Renaissance was introduced to Venice some fifty years after it had taken hold in the rest of Italy. The presbytery, with a triumphal arch leading to a cubic space, confirms the refined Lombardo style. The cupola, placed on pendentives surrounded by stone mouldings and decorated with a series of tondos depicting the evangelists, is based on Tuscan models, while the hemispheric form with eight little windows, is very probably a reworking of the Byzantine architecture that can be found in St Mark's. The light floods in to illuminate the main altar and the funeral stone for Doge Cristoforo Moro, who provided most of the money for the building. The interior, a vibrant symphony in white, originally contained altar-pieces by Giovanni Bellini and Carpaccio, since moved to the Accademia Galleries.

The majolica cupola in the Martini Chapel >

21 – Santa Maria dei Miracoli
1481 – 1494

The church was originally built to house the image of a *Madonna with Child* which was thought to have miraculous properties. The Lombardo family was entrusted with the project, which also included the nearby convent (almost totally destroyed in 1810) and the overhead walkway (no longer extant) once used by the nuns.

All four external sides of the splendid church can be seen, a rarity in the cramped spaces afforded by Venice, where, apart from St Mark's, no other church has been given such a privileged position, nor has any been built at the end of a wide street or in the middle of a square. Not only did

Detail of the base of a pilaster strip

the architects use this to full effect, but they also took full advantage of the adjacent canal, giving equal importance to all four façades. The decorative structure, which recalls the church of San Miniato in Florence, covers the entire outer surface and includes polychrome marbles which were chosen, cut, laid and inlaid with the greatest of care and with unbridled imagination. The prospect, which is hemmed in and crowned by the large semicircular, typically Venetian, pediment, is characterised by a large central rosette, around which there are alternated marble circles and round openings. The church is never clearly reflected in the water, but it does seem to "grow" out of it, with its purposefully elongated or deformed Ionic capitals.

The small bell tower, because of its irregular shape, expresses a completely different character if compared to the compact geometric composition of the church, and is therefore the least classical of the elements in the whole. The interior of the church, with its polychrome marble, basreliefs and statues, is intensely suggestive. There is only one central nave. The form of the church is rectangular, and the "boxed" ceiling is densely inlaid and contains fifty figures of prophets and patriarchs. The square presbytery, which is raised much higher than the level of the church, is flanked by two side tribunes with ambos – thus recalling the cathedral at Aquileia. The apse, which is introduced by an imposing arch exquisitely decorated in fruit and floral motifs, is crowned by a double spherical vault similar to St Mark's, which illuminates the miraculous image of Nicolò di Pietro. The pensile nuns' choir, placed above the entrance, is held up by pilasters decorated with bas-reliefs with floral and animal motifs, as well as sirens.

The stylistic eclecticism of the church makes it almost look like a little jewel box, and it is certainly one of the jewels of the Venetian Renaissance.

22 – San Giovanni Crisostomo
1497 – 1504

Originally built in the 11th century, when Venice was still partly Byzantine, this is one of the few churches in western Europe dedicated to the Patriarch of Constantinople. It was reconstructed by Codussi in 1497, and was given a three-part façade with a series of curvilinear crowning elements, essentially a reworking and honing of the San Michele in Isola façade. Although the materials used are much less prestigious (limestone and a reddish plaster), the overall effect is a rare example of equilibrium and coherence. The bell tower was demolished in 1532, when the *calle* was broadened. The church plan, a Greek cross inscribed within a square with a central cupola, was very dear to early Renaissance humanists and ultimately derived from early Byzantine forms (St Mark's is another example). The main "block" of the church was constructed according to precise proportions, dictated by the Platonic ideal according to which beauty is to be found in the simplicity and purity of geometric form. Four delicate pilasters delimit the main space, which, as in Santa Maria Formosa, is designed by the ribbings, giving rise to an extraordinary chiaroscuro effect on the white plaster finish. The severity of the Albertian forms introduced a proto-Renaissance type that was then used for many other Venetian churches.

The unusually-shaped main apse (a flat centre, giving onto the curved extremities), holds the elegantly harmonious *Altar-piece Depicting Saints* (1509) by del Piombo, his last work before moving to Rome. Giovanni Bellini's altar-piece, *St Jerome with Saints*, is also one of the artist's last works. Pervaded with a sense of humanity and serenity, the work deploys a "sunny" colour scheme which is very similar to Titian's style. The Tuscan-like framework and classical forms of Tullio Lombardo's large marble altar-piece, *The Crowning of the Virgin Mary* (1502), is testament to his adherence to humanist principles.

23 – Scalzi
1660 – 1689

The Carmelite Barefoot (or "Scalzi") order, established in 1633 in Venice after years of wandering around Italy, bought a large plot of cultivated land on which to build their first church, which was then dedicated to Our Lady of Nazareth in honour of a painting of the Virgin Mary which was originally on the island of Lazzaretto Vecchio. The building was enlarged in 1654 by Longhena, who was followed by the lay Carmelite Giuseppe Pozzo (responsible for the interior decorations) and Giuseppe Sardi (responsible for the grandiose façade). Despite its numerous statues and ornamentation, the façade is in fact one of the most "moderate" and balanced examples of Venetian Baroque. Facing directly onto the Grand

Canal, the façade's surface is covered in Carrara marble, and is divided into two orders formed by a series of paired columns framing the doorway and the niches with their statues (by Bernardo Falcone). The façade is rounded off by a triangular pediment, within which another, curvilinear pediment contains images of the Madonna and Child.

The planimetric plan put together by Longhena consists of a single nave with communicating side chapels. The central chapels, which are deeper than the others and which also extend into the church proper, form a sort of transept. Taken together, these chapels form a Greek cross. A large monumental arch leads to the raised presbytery and its cupola, behind which a row of columns lead to the choir. Pozzo transformed the church into an opulent Baroque masterpiece, adding a series of statues, polychrome and gilded decorations and various marble ornaments, all of which constitute a worthy example of how Baroque excess could be masterfully combined with sumptuous 18th century elegance. There are many references to Bernini in the very theatrical main altar (project by Pozzo), which recalls the baldachin in St Peter's in Rome, as well as in Meyring's *The Ecstasy of St Theresa* (1697). The remains of Venice's last Doge, Ludovico Manin, have been laid to rest in the Manin chapel, with its melodramatically overabundant decorations.

The vault, which was destroyed during an air-raid in 1915, originally contained a fresco by Tiepolo showing the Loreto family. Some of the sketches for the fresco and a few fragments can now be admired at the Accademia Galleries. However, there are a few Tiepolo frescoes in the Chapel of the Crucifix, as well as in the chapel dedicated to St Theresa of Avila, where the young artist cites Piazzetta, above all in the vivid flesh tones used for the subjects.

Detail showing decorative motif from Giuseppe Pozzo's main altar >

24 – Gesuiti
1715 – 1728

The entire complex was founded in the 12th century by the order of the *Crociferi*. The most important events in the history of this order, which was suppressed by Papal decree in 1656, can be seen in a cycle by Jacopo Palma the Younger, conserved in the small oratory in front of the church. The Jesuits, who, thanks to their role of privileged educators for the local nobility, quickly acquired enough power and prestige to deserve their own church, decided in 1715 to reconstruct the *Crociferi* church, which they had originally bought in 1657. This reconstruction, which was almost exclusively funded by the Manin family, was entrusted to Domenico Rossi, an architect who was very active at the time and who decided to remain faithful to the consolidated Latin cross plan typical of Jesuit churches in Rome.

The façade, erected in collaboration with the architect Giambattista Fattoretto, is rich in extremely plastic decorations. The lower order contains a series of enormous Corinthian columns which hold up the heavy and highly elaborate architrave and statues of the twelve Apostles. The doorway, framed by the playful perspectival view afforded by the columns, is surmounted by an interrupted tympanum containing marble figures brandishing the Manin family's coat-of-arms. The second order, in the centre of which there is an enormous window, is crowned by a triangular tympanum with a large representation of the Virgin ascending to heaven surrounded by a choir of angels. The angels' robes, flowing in an imaginary wind, add just the right emphatic touch to this dynamically dramatic example of Venetian Baroque.

The modest bell tower has maintained its original form, and is crowned by an 18th century belfry.

The grandiose interior of the church is striking in its almost bombastic and virtuoso-like marble decorations. Needless to say, there is nothing quite like it in Venice, and the green and white inlays covering the entire surface give the idea of a damask tapestry, which is further decorated with stuccoes, statues and gilding. An elaborate geometrical design continues in the priceless floor inlays. The overarching vault is equally elab-

orate, thanks to vividly-coloured Biblical stuccoes and frescoes by Fontebasso, one of the main exponents of the more excessive Baroque schools.

The single-nave plan, with a barrel vault and communicating side chapels, leads to a presbytery which is flanked by another two chapels. The two semicircular rooms with the chapels, to the side of the transept, also contain organs and choirs, their distinctive shape enhancing the acoustics. The abundant light also accentuates the brilliant nature of the decorations. The theatrical main altar by Pozzo is an imposing example of monumentality: the large baldachin, a glowing, gilded triumph of Baroque form, is held up by ten scrolled green marble columns covered in lapislazuli and leads upwards to a heavy, stuccoed cupola. The enormous 16th century funeral monument to Priamo da Lezze, with niches framed by pink marble columns, occupies the opposite wall and is a remnant from the old *Crociferi* church, as is the entire painting apparatus.

The Martyrdom of St Lawrence (1559) is one of Titian's last works, and expresses an anguished desperation in its highly dramatic nocturnal scene. The overall design of the painting seems to disintegrate, thus privileging the various pigments which, thickly layered onto the canvas, create magical, spectral effects. The cold light of the moon and the glowing torches underline the profound sense of death with which the entire painting is impregnated. *The Assumption of the Virgin Mary* (1555), painted by Tintoretto for the main altar of the original *Crociferi* church, is surprising in its use of lights and colours which force the observer to participate in the upwardly spiralling, ascending movement of the Virgin Mary.

25 – San Marcuola
1728 – 1736

The church, which was founded in the 9th century and reconstructed in the 12th, was completely restructured in the 18th century by Massari who, even though he maintained the original form of the building, moved the main façade so that it faced the Grand Canal. The prospect, which got no further than the base and the doorway, was to be very simple and straightforward, and very similar to the Gesuiti.

The interior, made all the more suggestive because of the dim lighting and the almost mathematical symmetry, gives the impression of a uniform space. It has only one square barrel vault nave leading to an apsed presbytery containing an elaborate 18th century altar. In the four corners of the church there are eight paired altars, each with marble states by Morlaiter substituting traditional altar-pieces. Baldachin pulpits have been placed above the doorways which, underlined by paired columns, are in the centre of the side walls with large rosettes. Massari's small chapel of Christ, placed where the original church portico was, is opposite the presbytery.

Amongst the many art works, perhaps the most interesting is Tintoretto's *Last Supper* (1547) which, despite the artist's youth, displays an incredible expressive force. Tintoretto's surprising originality is revealed in the violent lighting of the painting, which is the source of a profound energy that seems to invest the characters, illuminating their faces and giving them an almost frenzied vitality. The scene, which, according to medieval tradition, shows the characters face-on, is one of the artist's first versions of a theme that he was to work on quite often throughout his life.

26 – San Geremia
1753 – 1871

According to a stone inscription in the main doorway, the church was founded in the 11th century, reconstructed in 1292, demolished and subsequently completely rebuilt in its current form by the Brescian architect Carlo Corbellini in the 18th century. The marble façades, completed in 1871, are both flanked by the imposing 17th century Palazzo Labia and face onto two completely different urban situations: the *campo* in which a famous bull-hunt was held (perhaps because it was so close the Spanish Embassy), and the *rio* that gives onto the Grand Canal (from which you get a complete view of the building as a whole).

The prospect overlooking the *campo*, where the doorway is preceded by a very steep set of steps, is outlined by Corinthian pilasters which highlight the central body and hold up the arched tympanum, linked to the very close lateral wings by a series of curvilinear elements. The same motif, albeit simplified, can be found in the apse area on the Grand Canal side of the church, while the longer horizontal section along the *rio* is punctuated by a series of pilasters framing the three doorways with their overarching semicircular windows. These are grouped together to underline the central area, which is closed off by a curved pediment.

The 13th century brick bell tower, with Romanic two-light mullioned windows, has an Istrian stone belfry surmounted by an octagonal tambour (probably added in the Gothic period). The church itself has a Greek cross plan, with semicircular apses, a large oval cupola held up by groups of pilasters and surrounded by four little hemispheric cupolas. The church houses the body of St Lucy, patron saint of eyesight, who was brought to the church in 1863 from the unnamed Palladian church that was demolished to build the railway station. The Baroque interior also contains 18th century paintings.

27 – La Maddalena
From 1760

This small, refined construction, a masterpiece of Venetian Neo-classicism, was built over a pre-existing medieval complex which was demolished in the 18th century.

Tomaso Temanza, related to the Tirali family and Scalfarotto, put together the project. Temanza himself was a man of letters and a leading theorist in the field of new architectural language, and he based his projects on the rigorous geometric rules of the Classical period. The unitary nature of the "organism", as he had it, could rationally resolve the relationship between architecture and urban space. He thus came up with a perfectly cylindrical structure, covered with perfectly smooth, candid marble, and added a façade with an Ionic pronaos which was "flattened" onto the surface.

The interior, a hexagonal plan with a lowered cupola, is punctuated by paired columns and four symmetrical chapels framed by semicircular arches which are actually carved out of the wall. A very small cupola provides lighting for the oval presbytery, containing a very simple main altar. The use of priceless marbles and the architectural ideas in this small sacred space are a scaled-down reworking of the Pantheon, which is the model Temanza based himself on for the entire complex. The elegant building, where Temanza was buried in 1789, was completed by one of his students, Giannantonio Selva. Selva himself later drew up the project for La Fenice, continuing to interpret the Neo-classical norms that were to be swept away with the arrival of the French.

Sestiere di Dorsoduro e Giudecca

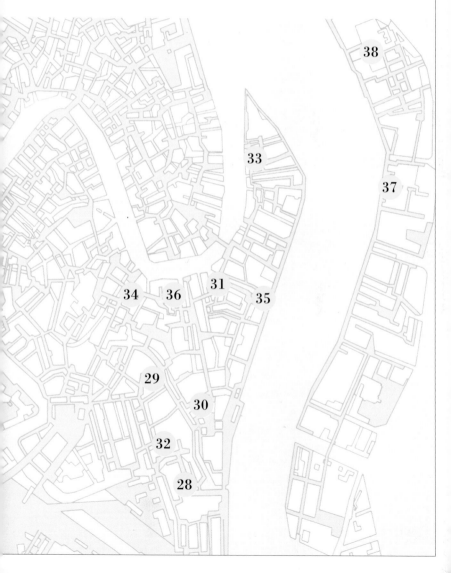

28 – San Nicolò dei Mendicoli
12th – 16th centuries

According to tradition, the church was founded in the 7th century in a very poor area of the city by Paduans fleeing from Longobard invaders. The poverty of the inhabitants not only suggested the name of the church (*"mendicoli"* in Venetian means "beggars"), but also "saved" the church from excessive restructuring over the years. It was reconstructed in the 12th century, and from then on it has maintained its bare sloping brick façade, and the characteristic raised arch two-light mullioned window is still extant. The little 15th century portico, which has disappeared from all churches except for San Giacomo at Rialto, was a meeting place for the *"pinzocchere"*, that is pious women who would gather there to pray. Until the 16th century, it was also used as a cemetery.

Alongside the church there is the imposing square Veneto-Byzantine bell tower, punctuated by pilaster strips. The bell tower has been dated to the 12th century.

The church's structure is that of a basilica, with three naves, a presbytery, semicircular apses framed by a 12th century Byzantine arch, and two side chapels. The columns, which were partially reworked in the 14th century, still show traces of their original colour, especially on the capitals. The two large pointed arches over the raised transept are also Gothic. The recently discovered *Crucifixion with Saints* belongs to the same period, and shows both Tuscan elements (especially in the way Christ is represented) as well as Byzantine touches (the procession of saints).

The interior of the church, which was completely reworked according to the Mannerist style in the 16th century, contains a rich array of paintings and sculptures. The central nave structure has an inlaid, gilded wooden covering, which contains scenes from the life of Christ (*The Resurrection* is by Palma the Younger) and statues of the apostles on the columns. On the iconostasis, the large wooden crucifix is placed between the Virgin Mary and John. The plain ceiling, which covers the original wooden truss beams, is divided into sections and contains friezes and paintings from the Veronese school. The monumental organ, with its gold inlays, is placed over the doorway, and dates from the 16th century. The floor, which was originally 30 cm under the level of the canals, was reconstructed and raised after the 1966 floods. The internal rooms all maintain their original proportions, which were based on precise numerical relationships, and give the building a sense of balance and harmony.

29 – I Carmini
13th – 14th centuries

This Gothic church, built by the Carmelite brothers in 1386, was originally much lower than it is now, as can be seen from the little arches along
the left side of the building. The Greek marble prothyrum which surrounds the side doorway is also from the 14th century. The cornice, with
its palm-tree and patera motif, is 13th century. The bell tower, which was
reconstructed in 1676, is topped off by a small octagonal temple with a
statue of the Madonna of Mount Carmel. The vast, solemn basilica-like
church has no transept, and is punctuated by a long series of twelve
columns with simple 14th century capitals. The columns separate the
three naves. The apses, which were reworked at the end of the 15th century, strike a carefully-planned balance between Renaissance decorative
elements and the overall Gothic structure. The 17th century ornamental
apparatus, based on a similar work in San Nicolò dei Mendicoli, hides the
pointed arches of the central nave. The wooden structure, painted and
gilded, also contains wooden statues of saints, prophets and historical figures, as well as twenty-four paintings depicting the history of the
Carmelite order. On the wall just inside the entrance there is a large
funeral monument to Jacopo Foscarini, a "sea captain" who died in 1602.
The monument is reminiscent of the Sansovino monument to Venier in
San Salvador. The church also contains two Renaissance altar-pieces:
Cima da Conegliano's *Nativity* (1509 – 1511), where an enchanting
rolling landscape is used as a backdrop to the sweetness and humanity of
the subjects; and the *Altar-piece of San Nicolò* (1529), by Lorenzo Lotto.
This was Lotto's first public commission in Venice, and was criticised as
"an example of terrible hues". The extremely detailed and suggestive
landscape, which is almost Nordic in style, is overshadowed by the monumental, and Titianesque, procession of saints.

30 – San Sebastiano
1508 – 1548

This Renaissance church, planned by Scarpagnino, faces the Rio of San Basilio. Its sloping prospect is divided into two orders and is closed off at its two ends by small paired columns and crowned by a large triangular pediment. The large central section is characterised by paired windows with triangular and circular windows flanking the doorway, with its curvilinear frontispiece, and by an "eye" in the upper register.

In the rectangular perimeter of the single-nave church, a Latin cross is formed by the choir, whose wings, sustained by three arches crowned by plutei, extend for two-thirds the length of the church and contain three chapels per side. The depth of the church delineates the vestibule, which is introduced by a transenna which is closed off on two sides by parapets and grates. The wooden organ and the enormous funeral monument by Sansovino lead to the raised presbytery which, in its turn, leads to the semicircular apse. Two minor chapels flank the apse. A large triumphal arch gives onto the large presbytery, underlined by an intense light that comes from the windowed tambour of the hemispheric cupola. The Lando chapel (to the left of the presbytery) has an odd glassed majolica floor, dated 1510, in the centre of which you can still see the commissioning family's coat-of-arms. The church, fascinating because of the clarity of its architectural language, also contains a spectacular cycle of paintings by Paolo Caliari, alias Veronese, whose trompe-l'œuil can easily be confused with real constructions. The artist, who was laid to rest at the foot of the organ, worked in the little church from 1551 to 1565, and it was here that he attained his full artistic maturity in terms of the luminosity of his colours, chiaroscuro technique and the divine serenity of his subjects. No artist has managed to infuse such energy into the robust plasticity of his figures.

31 – San Trovaso
1584 – 1657

The church, dedicated to Saints Gervase and Protase ("Gervasio" and "Protasio" in Italian – hence the hybrid form of "Trovaso"), was founded in the 9th century. It has since been reconstructed many times, the last being in 1584, when Francesco Smeraldi, one of Palladio's collaborators, was entrusted with the restoration. The building, which clearly harks back to Palladio in terms of overall design and architectural details, has two similar and equally important façades. They both have a double order and are flanked by tight wings delineated by a series of pilaster strips with Corinthian capitals, which are linked in the second order by a series of curvilinear elements. A triangular pediment crowns the two façades, which are characterised by a doorway and large rosette that occupies the entire central area in the upper order. The front façade gives onto a raised campo, while the other faces Rio San Trovaso. The bell tower, with its monumental belfry and octagonal tambour, can be found

Jacopo Tintoretto, *The Last Supper* (1564-1566)

next to this second façade. The Latin cross interior has only one nave with side chapels, an apsed presbytery and a vaulted ceiling. The 17th century pictorial apparatus includes late Veneto Mannerists such as Palma the Younger, Tintoretto and Malombra. However, the most important work is probably *Saint Chrysogonus on Horseback* by Michele Giambono, who was part of the international Gothic movement (active between 1420 and 1462) as well as Venice's official painter. In this vividly colourful painting, depicting the saint as a knight on his way to an unknown destination, Giambono has Chrysogonus pulling on the horse's reins, and seems to have placed the rider and his horse in almost too cramped a space. The saint's lance cuts across the scene diagonally, thus forming a clear division between the sacred and profane: on one side we have the saint's banner, with its red cross; on the other a wild, dark forest. The chapel of the Holy Sacrament, with its rich sculptural decorations, houses Tintoretto's *Last Supper* (1564 – 1566), a theme he often worked on. Here he expresses the choral message of poor, popular daily life: the objects, such as the wine flask and wicker chair in the foreground, and the naturalistically vivacious characters all indicate the lower classes. A touch of drama is added through the use of sudden shafts of light that illuminate the faces of the Apostles, thus underlining the theatrical nature of the scene. There is also another painting by Tintoretto, *The Temptations of St Antony* (1557), where he uses a multiplicity of lines to create a dynamic composition in which the plasticity of the figures is underscored by the use of chiaroscuro. The Clary chapel contains a splendid white marble altarfrontal showing a group of angels (1470). This is one of the most interesting examples of Renaissance sculpture, and has been attributed to the Donatello school.

Michele Giambono, *St Chrysogonus on Horseback* (detail) >

32 – Angelo Raffaele
1618 – 1639

According to tradition, this church, which is dedicated to the Archangel Raphael, was founded by St Magnus in the 7th century, although no written record has ever be found to confirm this. Despite the fact that the first document to mention the church is dated 1193, the 7th century is very likely right, as Venice was growing rapidly and assuming a much more important urban and political profile. The original Byzantine construction was demolished in the 17th century, as it was thought to be beyond repair. The project for its reconstruction was entrusted to Francesco Contin, and was to be in the Greek cross form with three equal façades underlining the church's urban role. This relationship between architecture and its surrounding space, however, would never be realised, and, due to a lack of funds, only one simple façade, facing the nearby canal, was completed in 1735.

Near the main portal we have a niche holding an image of the Archangel and Tobias, belonging to the Lombard school and dated to the 16th century.

The original Greek cross interior was reworked in the 18th century and given a presbytery flanked by two chapels and covered by a large cross-vault held up by pillars. Here we can find Fontebasso's beautiful 18th century fresco with its inlaid, gilded frame. Fontebasso was famous for his versatile style and striking colours, and was called to decorate the Winter Palace in St Petersburg.

The organ, which is placed over the entrance, has a splendid wooden balcony. Its five sections contain episodes in the life of Tobias by Gian Antonio Guardi, a refined exponent of the Venetian Rococo and brother of the landscape painter Francesco Guardi. In this work, the viewer is asked to admire the scintillating and transparent play of colours, which evoke a happy, light musicality.

33 – Santa Maria della Salute
1631 – 1681

On October 22, 1630, the government of the Serenissima Republic decided to build a votive temple dedicated to the Virgin Mary to celebrate the end of the Plague which had decimated more than a third of the Venetian population. The site chosen was one of the most prestigious, and the building, evoking the themes of heaven and water, was to be a symbol of victory over death and the rebirth of the republican city. Of the eleven projects presented, Baldassare Longhena's was considered the best, mainly because of the opulent magnificence of the language, which was seen as a stark contrast to the sober solidity of the Redentore that had been built only fifty years before.

In 1631, once the pre-existing religious complex known as the Trinity had been demolished, work began on the "round Baroque machination" which, with its conceptually innovative design, was to assume a specific meaning for Venice, underlining its symbolic function and acting as a visual link within the enormous void of St Mark's Basin. The church was given an octagonal form and raised almost theatrically onto a sort of platform preceded by a series of steps. This stupefying composition of volumes forms a "crown" that was supposed to refer directly to the crown worn by the Virgin Mary as an emblem of victory. The construction, externally punctuated by the prospects of the six chapels, has a grandiose Palladio-like façade dominated by a large cupola, surrounded by a flock of angels and sustained by eight robust pilasters and elegant spiral volutes.

The church is used each year for a procession during the Feast of the Salute, which is still one of the Venetians' favourite events. From the moment you enter the church you are overwhelmed by the church's spaciousness and luminosity. The space is defined by robust arches and composite pilasters sustaining the tambour of the cupola and separating the large nave from the ambulatory, onto which the various chapels face. Opposite the main entrance there is a large presbytery with side apses and covered by a smaller cupola. Here you will find the main altar, by Longhena, where the marvellous Byzantine icon, *The Image of the Virgin,*

is held. The complex plastic scenario is by Le Court and depicts Venice kneeling before the Virgin Mary vanquishing the Plague and surrounded by St Mark and Lorenzo Giustinian. Another incredible element is the polychrome marble floor, which extends in concentric waves from the central area, forming inlaid patterns in the shape of roses and Stars of David. The church also holds many paintings by Sassoferrato, Tintoretto and Luca Giordano. One of the six altars is adorned with Titian's *Pentecost* (1559), an enormous painting which was originally in the deconsecrated Santo Spirito church. In this Tintoretto-esque work, Titian uses his entire suggestive chromatic palette, using "explosions" of light to illuminate the monumental group of subjects. More works by Titian can be found in the sacristy. These are obviously from his mature period, as can be seen from the mobility of the characters, the audacious scenes and the Michelangelo-like plasticity, all of which reveal Titian's later abrupt conversion to a more markedly expressive mode.

34 – San Pantalon
1668 – 1686

The church, founded well before the 11th century, has undergone various re-workings. By the 16th century a portico running along the side facing the *campo* had been added. The church was later demolished. The rebuilding was entrusted to Francesco Comino, who turned the church ninety degrees so that the façade would give onto the *campo*. The high sloping prospect, with its large semicircular window, was never completed except for the main doorway and the side entrances.

The 18th century bell tower, attached to the church, has been attributed to Giovanni Scalfarotto. The church has one central nave, with three communicating side chapels and a plain presbytery. The slightly raised presbytery contains an imposing altar by Sardi (1671) surrounded by a panoply of little columns, capitals, wreaths of flowers, mirrors and polychromatic decorations. Fiumani's enormous pictorial composition (1680 – 1704) covering the ceiling is the largest canvas painting ever used for a ceiling and contains forty separate canvases mounted on boards. Fiumani gave full vent to his architectural imagination, placing architectural elements within a monumental Baroque scenery. Fiumani's painting takes up the form of the church, which he reworked by adding a large portico to the side of the building. The series of paintings is filled with a myriad of characters who are all linked to the life and martyrdom of the Saint, and, in the centre of the composition, in stark contrast with the sky behind him, we are offered an image of the Saint himself. The technique used by Fiumani constituted a break with Venetian tradition where all figures were seen from below and placed within garish gilded frames.

The Miracle of San Pantalon (1587), in the San Pantalon chapel, is one of Veronese's last works, and is an example of his later, more meditative and melancholic style. The colours are merely adumbrated, the hues darker and more sombre, and his formerly clear skies have given way to the artificial lighting of interiors. The Sacro Chiodo ("Sacred Nail") chapel is so called because it contains a relic of one of the nails used for the Crucifixion. The chapel also contains Giovanni d'Alemagna and Antonio Vivarini's *Crowning of the Virgin* (1444), depicting a series of

saints within an overwhelming decorative scenery, and a 14th century triptych attributed to Paolo Veneziano.

Pietro Longhi, famous for his miniatures of everyday life, painted a series of frescoes for the church between 1744 and 1745, bringing to bear the deft touch of a miniaturist in a series of life-size images.

35 – Gesuati
1726 – 1736

The Dominicans took over the church which had formerly belonged to the Company of the Gesuati, suppressed by Papal edict in 1668, and built the current church alongside the earlier Renaissance construction. Giorgio Massari's project harks back to Palladio, and especially San Giorgio and the Redentore. The prospect, facing the Zattere, is made up of one single order which is divided into three sections by enormous Corinthian columns sustaining the large jutting cornice and the triangular tympanum. The simple raised doorway, with a marble cornice and memorial stone, is flanked by niches containing statues. Two small bell towers can be found at the extremity of the nave area. The elegant interior, with a series of communicating side chapels, has a single rectangular nave which leads to the presbytery, over which there is a cupola, designed so as to

provide as much light as possible. The majestic main altar is surrounded by a semicircle of columns surrounding the lapislazuli tabernacle. The altar is surmounted by a curvilinear tympanum, which also separates the exedra choir from the presbytery. The accentuated trabeation adds to the sense of movement and light, and the church is one of the most coherent and refined examples of Rococo in Venice. The ivory and silvery grey colours are further enriched by the marble inlays of the floor design and the rich imaginative style Mortelier deployed for his statues and reliefs. The church is made all the more interesting by the Tiepolo frescoes which, placed within polychrome stucco frames, decorate the vault and depict *Episodes from the Life of St Dominic* and *The Institution of the Rosary* (1737 – 1739). Tiepolo, who was influenced by Ricci, adapted themes dear to Veronese, and his compositions are immersed in a divine light and almost surreal architectural elements contrasted against multi-coloured skies. Along with the frescoes used to decorate the presbytery, Tiepolo also painted the altar-piece, *Three Dominican Saints* (1748), where the Virgin Mary, seraphically seated amongst the clouds, seems to be protecting the group of saints singing a joyful hymn. In the *Three Saints* altar-piece by Piazzetta (1739), the forcefully expressive characters are depicted through the use of a colour scheme whose sobriety almost verges on the monochrome. Sebastiano Ricci's *Pious V and Saints* (1732 – 1734) is one of his later works, and the re-elaboration of a Veronesian theme is an excellent example of mature Rococo, a masterful blend of perspectival images as a backdrop to lightly traced figures highlighted by a transparent luminosity.

Giambattista Tiepolo, *The Institution of the Rosary* (1737-1739) >

36 – San Barnaba
1749 – 1776

According to tradition, the church was originally founded in the 9th century. It was subsequently rebuilt in the 14th century, only to be demolished again in the 18th as it was thought to be dangerous. The current building was entrusted to Lorenzo Boschetti, one of Massari's followers, and is a reworking of the Gesuati church.

The classical façade in Istrian stone, punctuated by Corinthian columns and surmounted by a triangular tympanum, has a side strip of grouped columns and pilasters. This heavy, static mass, with its large doorway and empty niches, looms over the campo with its polished uniformity.

The bell tower was erected right next to the nearby bridge in the year 1000 and is one of the oldest in Venice. It has a typically squared form, with pilaster strips and an open belfry with three-light mullioned windows. The cone-shaped spire with angular pinnacles was added in the 14th century, when the church was first restructured.

The church's interior, covered with frescoes from the Tiepolo school, has a single nave and three side altars. The square presbytery is covered by a cross-vault. The church contains two paintings by Palma the Younger. Despite the fact that he was one of Titian's students, these particular paintings are more indebted to Michelangelo, and are almost Mannerist in style.

37 – The Redentore
1577 – 1592

The church, originally built as a votive temple to commemorate the end of the 1576 Plague, is visited by Venetians each year during the third Sunday in July. The Republican government commissioned Palladio to build the church, even though it was completed by Da Ponte. This magnificently symbolic building faces onto the Giudecca canal. The geometry of the façade, whose calibrated sense of proportion corresponds to the interior design of the church, is a re-elaboration of the classical forms used in the many Palladian villas in the Veneto. On a tall stylobate there are a series of columns which, in their central section, delineate the form of a temple surmounted by a triangular tympanum. At the top of a lengthy flight of steps we have a large doorway that takes up the design of the façade and is flanked by two niches containing statues by Gerolamo Campagna. The lateral wings, corresponding to the chapels, are almost moved into the background and set within paired pilasters and portions of tympana. The immense cupola, flanked by two small bell towers, dominates the entire church.

The solemn interior, lit by enormous windows, is in the form of a Latin cross. There is only one, very wide nave with a truss vault, with three communicating chapels per side. The chapels are underlined by the large arches, and are separated by series of paired semi-columns. The raised presbytery is developed within the vast apsed transept and leads to an exedra colonnade, beyond which is a very deep-set choir. The isolated main altar, used for all sacred functions, has been given a large Baroque tabernacle and bronze statues by Campagna. The church contains works by Vivarini, Jacopo and Francesco Bassano, Veronese and Saraceni, thanks to whose *The Ecstasy of St Francis* the Caravaggio style was introduced to Venice.

38 – The Zitelle
1582 – 1586

This is the third Palladian church in Venice, even though it was completed by Jacopo Bozzetto on Palladio's death. It is almost an optical extension of the prospect of San Giorgio, and along with the Redentore it forms a very interesting triptych that qualifies the St Mark's Basin area.

The church was dedicated to the Visitation of the Virgin Mary, and three of its sides are surrounded by the Zitelle (or "Old Maids'") hospice, so called because, in the 18th century, poor yet virtuous young ladies were placed in the hospice, and they became famous for their elaborate and intricate lacework and musical activity.

The finely-honed architectural complex, with its classical composure, is surmounted by a large cupola. It has a marble façade made up of two orders, which are surrounded by two pairs of pilaster strips. The entire structure is topped off by a triangular tympanum, on the sides of which there are two robust bell towers. The large central window is flanked by a series of smaller windows which give onto the doorway and illuminate the simple interior.

The single room of the interior, covered by the large cupola, is square, but the otherwise severe angles have been smoothed down to enhance the acoustics. A small, slightly raised presbytery and two small side choirs (which can be reached directly from the adjacent convent) give onto the nave, which is preceded by a barrel vaulted atrium.

The altars contain 16th century paintings by Francesco Bassano, the Vassilacchis and Palma the Younger. Palma's *Oration in the Garden* includes portraits of the commissioners Pasquale and Elisabetta Foppa, who are buried in the church.

Sestiere di Castello

Building not in map

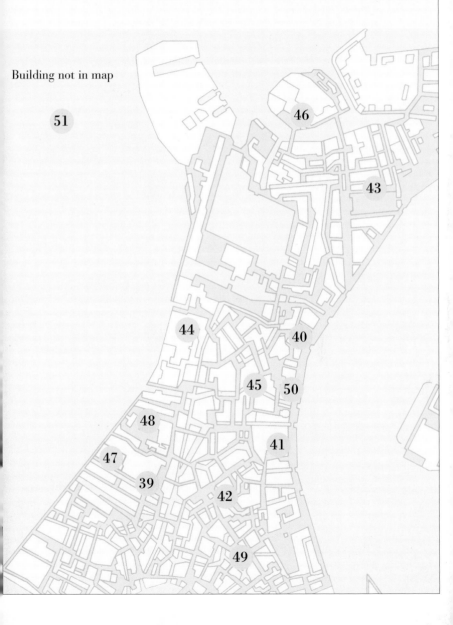

39 – San Zanipolo
14th – 15th centuries

The church was built in 1246 on a plot of land given to the Dominican Brothers by Doge Jacopo Tiepolo. It was subsequently completed in the 14th century in Gothic style, based on the Latin cross schemes used for convent basilicas. Consecrated in 1430, it was called the Pantheon of the Serenissima as many Doges were buried in the church. Over 100 metres long and 42 high, it is the largest Gothic church in Venice, and is similar to the Frari. The verticality of the brick façade, with pilaster strips forming three sections, is balanced by the use of deep pointed-arch niches (holding Gothic and early Christian urns) in the lower order. The marble doorway, made after 1459 by Bartolomeo Bon, unites Gothic and Renaissance elements, and is framed by paired columns in groups of two, originally used for the Torcello church. Alongside the doorway there are two 13th century Byzantine statues of the Virgin Mary and the Annunciating Angel, while the pilasters contain marble slabs, Veneto-Byzantine paterae and a marble bas-relief with Greek inscriptions, perhaps dating from the 6th century. The unfinished façade, evoking the interior of the church and its three naves, is crowned by marble aediculae with statues and spires. The absence of a bell tower gives the church its own unique presence within the urban landscape. The imposing cross-vaulted central nave is surrounded by enormous columns, linked by wooden tie-beams, separating it from the two minor side aisles containing the chapels. There is a polygonal apse within the transept, along with four minor chapels. The marked verticality of the interior gives the sense of the "immensity" of the church, which is further enhanced by the exceptional lighting in the main apse, which is surrounded by a sequence of windows and rosettes. The large vividly-coloured stained glass window is one of the few surviving examples of Murano production between the Gothic and early Renaissance periods. The overall space, which has been interpreted in a typically "Veneto" style, contrasts with the half-shadows so much in vogue in medieval churches on the mainland.

In Giovanni Bellini's early *Polyptych of St Vincenzo Ferreri* (1465), light is again the protagonist, surrounding and linking the characters. In *St*

Antony Begging, especially painted for the church by Lotto in 1542, the Titianesque cherubs, counterposed with the crowd of postulants immersed in the shadows, create a rare sense of pathos. The ceiling of the San Domenico chapel, with its delicate chiaroscuro tones used as inspiration by the young Tiepolo, was painted by Piazzetta some time after 1725.

The *Monument to Doge Pasquale Mocenigo*, a masterpiece by the Renaissance architect and sculptor Lombardo, is a sort of lay commemoration of the Doge. There are indeed sacred figures, but the profane elements predominate, and even Mocenigo himself, astride the sarcophagus, seems larger-than-life. At a formal level, Lombardo cites both Florentine art and Rizzo's *Monumento Tron* which can be found at the Frari. The Rosary chapel, opened in 1575 after Venice's victorious Battle of Lepanto, was restored after the fire of 1867. Based on a project by Vittoria, who added Michelangelo-like statues during his Mannerist phase, it was originally a sort of jewel case full of rare and precious gems. The walls have sumptuous wooden ornamental covers, attributed to Piazza, and a magnificently inlaid gilded wooden ceiling containing three paintings by Veronese originally found in the church of Umiltà. These paintings, respectively *The Assumption of the Virgin Mary*, *Herdsmen Adoring the Virgin* and *The Annunciation*, are all imbued with a joyous light that illuminates sumptuously-construed buildings and figures pervaded by a sense of contemplative serenity.

Lorenzo Lotto, *St Anthony Giving Alms* (1542) >

40 – San Giovanni in Bragora
15th century

The church, perhaps founded as early as the 8th century, is dedicated to St John the Baptist, whose body was brought to Venice from the East. The term *"bragora"* is of uncertain origins, but some think it is a corruption of two old words in Venetian, *"brago"* and *"gora"* (respectively, "mud" and "stagnant canal"); on the other hand, some maintain that the word derives from *"bragolare"* ("to fish"), or even from the Greek *"agora"* ("public square"). The often-restored church was completely rebuilt in 1475.

The unadorned tripartite façade, with a large central arch and curvilinear linking elements, is in a transitional style between late Gothic and Renaissance, introducing elements that Codussi would later use for San Zaccaria and San Michele in Isola. Inside the church there is quite a clear break between the three-naved Gothic structure, without a transept but with a wooden truss ceiling, and the 1490 presbytery, which is clearly early Renaissance in form and style. Just under the last span of the central nave you will notice that the floor is slightly raised, indicating that this was probably the original location for the choir (demolished in the 18th century). The original marble wall coverings from the choir can still be seen around the main altar. Remains of the 15th century frescoes can still be seen along the side aisles and on the large arch in the apse area. The very contained and suggestive interior, which contains a wealth of works of art, is filled with a terse light that seems to filter in from the altar-piece in the main chapel – Cima da Conegliano's *Baptism of Christ* (1492-95). The scene contains one of the artist's favourite elements, a hilly landscape, and the characters, depicted in enamel-like colours, seem to be crystallised in the silence of an immobile nature. Conegliano also painted the *Saints Constantine and Helen* altar-piece (1501 – 1503), which is further proof of Venice's devotion to the Roman emperor.

Cima da Conegliano, *The Baptism of Christ* (1492-1495)

41 – San Zaccaria
1444 – 1500

The enormous wealth and prestige of the monastery have made it a refined *locus* for the Venetian patrician class. The campo it faces onto was considered private property, and the two entrances were closed after dark. The arches of the 16th century cloister to the left of the building are placed over the original convent cemetery while, to the right, you can see the façade of the original 9th century church. The prospect was completed in 1481 by Codussi, who gave a Renaissance touch to the late Gothic architecture. The façade is built over the original stylobate, which is covered in High Gothic polychrome stripes and panels. Curved buttresses and string-courses on a horizontal axis contain the semicircular pediment, a recurrent element in Codussi's projects. The architectural apparatus is "lightened" by columns, which give the façade a sense of plasticity and playful contrasts between light and shade. The Veneto-Byzantine bell tower dates from the 13th century.

All that is left of the original 9th century construction is a fragment of a floor mosaic in the San Tarasio chapel, where a gothic apse was added in the 15th century. Around the 10th-12th centuries, a Romanic church was built over the Byzantine basilica.

A suggestive crypt, a section of floor mosaic from the altar area and remains of a fresco are the only remnants of this Romanic church. The restructuring project, begun in 1443, was entrusted to Antonio Gambello who came up with the idea of a large, three-naved structure, with a series of chapels "radiating" from a pentagonal apse and a deambulatory. The layout is very rare in Italy and the only one of its kind in Venice. The robust columns, which separate the naves and hold up the large semicircular arches, are surmounted by eagles with their wings spread. The lunettes, showing scenes from the life of the Doges, is testimony to the very close relationship between the Benedictine monastery and Palazzo Ducale. The presbytery area, was built under the large cupola, which is surrounded by five smaller cupolas.

The beautiful church also contains important works of art, such as the light-filled *Sacred Conversation* (1505), one of Giovanni Bellini's mature

works and an exquisite example of his use of colour. The altar-piece is part of the altar proper and creates a perfect perspectival fiction.

The San Tarasio chapel contains three polyptyches by Vivarini and d'Alemagna, which are complex, late-Gothic altar-pieces painted on gilded wood, with impressive frames sculpted with marvellous architectural motifs. Before his twentieth birthday, the Florentine painter, Andrea del Castagno, one of Masaccio's followers, painted the fresco *The Church Fathers* onto the vaulting cells of the chapel.

The figures, which almost seem to be carved out of stone, are given an aggressive force that indicates an extraordinary energy. The Sant'Atanasio chapel houses the wooden choir, which was restored in the 16th century, and Tintoretto's *Birth of St John* altar-piece.

42 – Santa Maria Formosa
1492 – 1604

According to popular tradition, the Virgin Mary appeared to St Magnus in the form of a splendid, buxom (*"formosa"* in Italian) woman, and asked him to build a church just under a cloud. Thus the first Venetian church dedicated to the Virgin Mary was built, and instead of being called Santa Maria della Purificazione (its original name), it was called Santa Maria Formosa. Founded in the 7th century and reconstructed many times, Mauro Codussi planned the current church. It might well be defined his first masterpiece, and it certainly is one of the most original churches of the early Renaissance because of its unitary style. The exterior, unfortunately, lacks the same unitary style, as Codussi died in 1504,

when the two façades had only just been begun. Later, the Cappello family funded the finishing work which, as they wanted a sort of homage to the family itself, completely modified the original plan.

The classical façade giving onto the rio, erected in 1542, was dedicated to the "sea captain" Vincenzo Cappello, who had defeated the Turks, while the façade giving onto the campo, erected in 1604, contains portraits of members of the Cappello family. The bell tower is also from the 17th century, and its entrance is surmounted by an extremely expressive marble mask.

The interior of the church more or less maintained the pre-existent Greek cross form, which gives a clear and dominant feel to the entire construction. However, when the wings off the central nave were slightly lengthened, the plan was transformed into a Latin cross with three vaulted naves. The stone ribbing along the walls, the only ornamentation in Brunelleschi style, stands out against the white plaster and almost looks like a very subtle yet sturdy armour underlining the rigour and functionality of the structures. The various spaces and rooms within the church cannot be seen from one single vantage point, but, despite the complexity of the composition, they do not give the impression being disorganised or lacking in consistency. The entire church is bathed in a terse, sensual light. The cupola was very carefully rebuilt in 1921, after the church had been bombed by the Austrians.

Many artisan guilds worked directly in the church, amongst which the Scuola dei Casselleri (makers of dowry chests) and the Scuola dei Bombardieri (ship builders). The altar dedicated to this latter group contains an altar-piece by Palma the Elder, *The Polyptych of St Barbara* (1523), patron saint of the Bombardieri. Vivarini painted an exquisite *Madonna of Mercy* (1473), which graces a very refined marble altar as if it were a precious inlay.

Bartolomeo Vivarini, *Madonna of the Misericordia* (1473) >

144

BARTHOLOMEVS VIVARIIVS DE
MVRIANO PINXIT AVCCCCLXXIII

43 – San Giuseppe
1512

This small church (architect unknown) is part of a vast convent in the popular Castello area of Venice. The monastery, which first belonged to the Augustinian order of nuns and then the Salesians, is built around three successive cloisters where, despite the various restorations, you can still make out the original 16th century plan. The church was built along the canal, and the side of the church adjacent to the canal has a double

row of pilaster strips interrupted by a series of windows. The simple sloping façade, delimited by pairs of pilaster strips and topped off with a triangular tympanum, has a series of elongated windows and a small central eye. The only decorative element is a marble covering, or pseudo-façade, at the centre of which is the main doorway with its pilasters, side niches and a tympanum decorated with bas-reliefs depicting the *Adoration of the Magi* by Giulio del Moro.

The interior has only one nave, with a presbytery flanked by two chapels. It maintains the typically contemplative feel of convent churches. The plain ceiling, partly frescoed by Torriglia in the 17th century, has a *St Joseph in Glory*, framed by columned architectural perspectives. The wall next to the entrance still has the original, characteristic wooden pensile choir used by the nuns, and there are two 16th century pensile organs over the apse chapels. The organs are decorated with inlays and pictorial motifs. The Grimani family monument, in the presbytery, contains Veronese's *Adoration of the Shepherds* (1582 – 1583). In the left of the painting there is a portrait of Gerolamo Grimani in priestly garb. Most interesting are the purposefully dark, sombre colours, used by Veronese in his mature period to give a sense of authentic religiosity.

The enormous funeral monument to Doge Marino Grimani and his wife Morosina Morosini is a late 16th century work by the architect Vincenzo Scamozzi. The marble figures and bronze reliefs are by Gerolamo Campagna. Over the classical, almost pompous architectural apparatus there is a large relief depicting *The Virgin Mary with Child Being Adored by the Doge and His Wife*.

Giovanni Antonio Torriglia, *The Glory of St Joseph* (17th century) >

44 – San Francesco della Vigna
1530 – 1572

Founded in 1253 on the site of a vineyard donated by the son of the Doge
Ziani to the local monks, the church was reconstructed in the 16th century according to a project by Sansovino, and might well be considered
the first example of Renaissance architecture in Venice. Palladio's façade
(1569) is in the form of a Greek temple. Along the base there are a series
of Corinthian semi-columns with pseudo-pronaos, leading to a triangular
tympanum at the centre of which there is a rounded bas-relief depicting
an eagle, symbol of Christ and Divine Knowledge. The extremely high
doorway, framed by two columns and a curvilinear strip of marble with
concentric rays, is surmounted by a cambered window and surrounded
by geometric panels and two niches containing bronze statues by Aspetti.

The pursuit of classical form, a mainstay of Palladio's work, can also be found in Palladio's other Venetian churches - San Giorgio and the Redentore.

The 16th century bell tower, reworked in the 17th, is one of the tallest in the city. The interior of the Latin-cross church has a single wide nave with raised side chapels. The nave, however, has been extended along the transept to form a "T", a symbol of perfection and salvation. The deep, squared presbytery, separated from the choir by the main altar, is flanked by two side chapels and houses the funeral monument to Andrea Gritti. The unadorned style of the church belies its complex organisation, which is the end result of a debate promoted by Prior Francesco Ziani's study on harmonious neo-Platonic proportions. In fact, the sense of equilibrium many feel on entering the church is due to the fact that the church was organised according to the mystical qualities of the number three. The intellectualistic interior also contains works by Vivarini, Giorgione, Veronese, Palma the Younger and Giovanni Bellini. But the most interesting is without doubt a *Madonna with Child* (1463-69), the only work by Brother Negroponte. The uniqueness of the work derives from the fact that, even though he was working in the full flush of the Renaissance, he offered a collation of late-Gothic motifs. The painting, which also makes use of painted paper inserts, depicts a Madonna wearing a luxurious brocade gown, surrounded by flowers and seated on a throne bearing classical bas-reliefs which rework Paduan and Mantegna motifs. The so-called *Giustinian Altar-Piece* (1515), in the Giustinian chapel, was Veronese's first commissioned work in Venice, and introduced him to the nobility of the Serenissima, who then made him their privileged artist. Although he reworked the Titianesque scheme of the *Pesaro Altar-Piece* at the Frari, Veronese added his own combination of pure luminous hues as well as graphic novelties based on the Mannerist style.

Antonio Falier da Negroponte, *Madonna with Child* (1463-1469 >

45 – San Giorgio dei Greci
1539 – 1571

At the end of the 15th century, there were about 4,000 members of the Greek community in Venice. Most were publishers, artists and writers, and they were given permission to build their own school and church, which is still used today for Greek Orthodox services. The original project was by Sante Lombardo, but the church was completed by Gianantonio Chiona and consecrated in 1561. The two adjacent 17th century constructions are by Longhena. They are Palazzo Flanghinis, now a Museum of Byzantine icons, and the Scuola di San Nicolò, currently the Greek Cultural Institute.

The church's tripartite structure, animated by a series of rosettes and shell-decorated niches, is concluded by a triangular tympanum.

The leaning bell tower contains a few remnants from the old Renaissance portico and small loggia.

The late-Renaissance church has only one nave, a central hemispheric cupola and a women's gallery over the main entrance. The sumptuous interior is made all the livelier by the Greek Orthodox iconostasis which, gleaming with its decorations, separates the nave from the choir. The precious icons are the work of the 16th century Crete painter Damaskinos. The church also houses an priceless icon of *Christ the Pantocrator* (14th century), brought to Venice from Constantinople just before the fall of the Byzantine Empire.

This unique religious building contains works by Greek artists who, in the 16th and 17th centuries, revolutionised the traditionally static nature of Byzantine art by introducing a specifically Venetian colour scheme. Of these painters, the most important is without doubt Dominikos Theotokopulos, also called El Greco.

46 – San Pietro in Castello
1557 – 1621

The basilica was built on the small island of Olivolo ("Olive Grove"), or Castello ("Castle"), which has been inhabited since the 5th century. The church was erected and dedicated to St Peter in 841, and substituted the original 7th century church dedicated to Saints Serge and Bacchus. It was originally also a bishop's residence until, in 1451, it became the Venetian Patriarch's home. It was a cathedral until 1897, when the title was given to St Mark's. In 1556, the Patriarch Vincenzo Diedo commissioned Palladio to rebuild the medieval construction. Contrary to procedure, Palladio began with the façade, but work came to a halt on the death of Diedo. The prospect was completed at the end of the century by Smeraldi (called Fracao), who carefully followed the Palladian project. The rest of the building was subsequently completed by Grapiglia. The candid façade in Istrian stone, with a double superimposed framework that

seems to be a citation of the Redentore façade, is a reflection of the three-nave interior.

The Istrian stone bell tower by Codussi (1482) is "powerful, isolated, crystal-white. Immobile at its base, yet in movement up there amongst the clouds [...] It is a sculpture, caught between entrapment and flight [...] ready to flee with the wind" (P Barbaro).

The planimetric Latin cross scheme with a truncated transept covered by an extremely high cupola leads to an apsed presbytery introduced by a large arch and flanked by two side chapels. The broad central nave, delimited by the arches that punctuate a succession of side chapels, gives the church a sense of almost limitless space. The cathedral, bringing together classical form and Baroque imagination, constitutes a turning point between the 16th and 17th centuries. The main altar (1649), with its theatrical architectural form and sculptural additions, holds the remains of Lorenzo Giustinian (later beatified) and has all the form of an imposing Baroque "machine". It is the work of Clemente Moli, based on a design by Longhena. Pellegrini's coloured Rococo narrative cycle of the life of St Peter lines the presbytery and culminates in the bright luminosity of the apotheosis (in the vault of the apse). Longhena also projected the Vendramin chapel, which is covered in priceless marble and Baroque statues, and also contains a remarkable altar-piece by Luca Giordano. The church also has a miniature Cathedral of St Peter of Antioch (842-867), made of various pieces of marble, which the Eastern Emperor Michele Paleologo gave to the Doge of Venice.

Baldassarre Longhena and Clemente Moli, *Main Altar* (1649) >

47 – San Lazzaro dei Mendicanti
1601 – 1649

From as early as the 13th century, the hospital dedicated to St Lazarus (the patron saint of lepers) was looking after people suffering from leprosy and, over the centuries, it also began to take in beggars, the poor in general and then also young girls from the lower classes. These were taught a trade and given a musical education. The current set of buildings, based on a project by Scamozzi, is based on the Zitelle: the church, closed off on two sides by the hospice, has a neo-Palladian façade designed by Sardi in 1673. The classically-inspired prospect, from the high base with Corinthian columns holding up the jutting cornice crowned by the triangular pediment, has only one Baroque element - the doorway, with its curvilinear tympanum. The interior is characterised by an imposing and heavy-handed monument to Alvise Mocenigo, who defended Candida from the Turks. The monument was designed by Sardi in 1658, and was given an exquisitely Baroque decoration. Almost as if it were a second façade, the monument separates the church from the vast vestibule which was designed to block out all noise from the outside during the young women's recitals. In the prospect, divided into two orders, there are a series of sculptures by Le Court, amongst which the most interesting is the monumental figure of Mocenigo himself. The church has only one nave, covered by a vault and lit from the large windows, which leads to the square presbytery. Along the side walls there are a series of raised stages which can be reached directly from the adjacent hospice. The church houses Guercino's only Venetian painting, *St Helen Adoring the True Cross*, which, with its references to Caravaggio, brought new life to Venetian art. Works by Tintoretto and Veronese are also held in the church, including the latter's *Crucifixion*, which is one of the most movingly melancholic works he has ever undertaken.

48 – Ospedaletto
1667 – 1674

The church, founded in 1527, is popularly called "Ospedaletto" (which in Venetian means "little hospital or hospice"), deriving from the fact that it was right next to a hospice for the infirm, the elderly and poor women who, apart from being taught a trade, were also given music and singing lessons. After centuries of concerts in the church, in the 18th century the very much appreciated women's choir moved to the elegant "music room" within the hospice. The room was frescoed by Guaranda, and contains a series of small choirs hidden behind a series of beautiful grates. Very little remains of the 17th century restructuring by Giuseppe Sardi except for the oval staircase in the hospice. Longhena complete the restoration work, and in 1670 he put up the façade for the pre-existing church. This imposing construction is characterised by the tormented caryatids in the second order (by Le Court) which hold up the trabeation surmounted by the statue-laden attic. The sculptural emphasis of the Baroque façade, rich in architectural framework and enlivened by a series of masks, is unique in Longhena's long production. It was here, in fact, that he first used decorations normally reserved for the interior of a church on the outside as well. In the church itself, the architect used magnificent marble altars instead of the traditional wooden ones, erected the main altar and extended the choir, decorating it with wooden sculptures and very refined grates. The plain ceiling was frescoed in 1907 by Cherubini. The church contains *The Sacrifice of Isaac*, one of Tiepolo's early works. In this highly dramatic painting, Tiepolo makes use of the menacing chiaroscuro technique introduced by Piazzetta, his first master.

49 – Santa Maria della Fava
1705 – 1753

The church, originally built to house a putatively miraculous image of the Virgin Mary, is popularly called "La Fava" after the name of the rich family who lived in the vicinity. The church was demolished in the early 1700s, and the area became the churchyard of the current church, which was designed by Antonio Gaspari. The architect's was an innovative "Roman" project, inspired by Borromini, and included a very lively curvilinear façade with a markedly jutting doorway, two small bell towers and a high cupola. The design, which was not appreciated in a Venice that had embraced Palladio as the only norm, was subsequently scaled down. The unadorned prospect, which, except for the doorway, remained unfinished, looms over the little campo with its radically vertical form. The elegant interior, originally planned to have an oval form, has a single, rounded nave with three side chapels separated by septa and punctuated by Corinthian pilasters containing niches with statues by Marchiori and Morlaiter, the best sculptors in Venice at the time. In 1750 Giorgio Massari was called on to complete the church, and he was responsible for the presbytery and the covering. Of the noteworthy 18th century paintings lining the altars, the most interesting are Jacopo Amigoni's *Visitation* (the clear and lively colours give the painting its delicate Rococo flavour), and Piazzetta's *Virgin with Child and St Philip Kneeling in Prayer*. When Piazzetta died a pauper, he was buried in the Albrizzi family tomb (to the right of the nave). The church also houses Tiepolo's marvellous *The Education of the Virgin Mary* (1732-1733), where the artist deploys delicate pastels to depict Mary as a young girl, in sharp contrast with the chromatically vigorous colours used for her parents.

50 – Pietà
1744 – 1760

The 16th century Hospice for poor orphan girls is one of the Serenissima's many works of public charity, and, like the Zitelle and Ospedaletto, the *putte ospealere*, i.e. "hospice girls", were given a musical education. In 1735 a competition was held for a reconstruction project for the entire building complex, won by Massari. However, only the church was completed. The classically neo-Palladian façade, finished in 1906, is a tripartite structure with enormous Corinthian semi-columns on a high base. The triangular tympanum was placed over the columns, and the central doorway, introduced by a short flight of steps, is flanked by windows and refined geometric decorations. The harmonious interior perfectly mixes functionality and the religious demands of the various rooms. The vast hall, preceded by an atrium designed to sound-proof the church, has an elliptical form culminating in the presbytery, and has a lowered vaulted ceiling, again designed to enhance the acoustics. Paired pilasters give rhythm to the walls, which contain altars surmounted by windows and pensile choirs with wrought iron grates and decorated parapets. Here the girls' choirs, directed by Benedetto Marcello and Vivaldi (who wrote most of his compositions for this institution), would entertain the nobility of Venice at the peak of its splendour. The church, in fact, is a splendid "concert hall", and was frescoed by Tiepolo himself. In his work for the church, Tiepolo brought to bear the most delicate of Rococo decorative detail and created one of the masterpieces of 18th century Venetian art. His *Crowning of the Virgin Mary* (1754-55), a sumptuous ceiling fresco, depicts the triumph of celestial music, and the ascending structure of the work's complex orchestration is almost the painterly equivalent of Vivaldi's own crescendos.

Giambattista Tiepolo, *The Coronation of the Virgin Mary* (1754-1755) >

51 – San Michele in Isola
1469 – 1478

When the Camaldolese monks decided to reconstruct the crumbling 13th century buildings on the small island of San Michele, they called on the young Mauro Codussi. Codussi gave full vent to his genius in adapting Tuscan styles to the lagoon's Gothic forms. Even though the tripartite façade, with its curvilinear counterforts and tympanum, is typically Venetian, the architectural "vocabulary" used is highly innovative. The forms and volumes are regulated by mathematical principles; rigorous proportion gives the idea of perfect equilibrium. The strong unitary sense

of the project meant that each individual element could be included only insofar as it was related to the whole. The fragments of a circle that conclude the prospect, in their carefully-planned "imperfection", give a dynamic touch to the structure, whose curved lines are a conscious citation of the large lunettes used for St Mark's and Alberti's *Tempio Malatestiano* in Rimini. The smoothed keystones in Istrian stone, jutting cornices and shell decorations are used to give movement and life to the façade which, in its unpretentious candour, is one of the lagoon's masterpieces.

The Gothic bell tower, with baked brick cupola and decorations, is the epitome of elegance.

The interior of the church, organised according to the principles of clarity and simplicity, has three naves, separated by broad arches and covered by a coffered ceiling. A triumphal arch leads to the square presbytery, with a semicircular apse flanked by two small chapels. The apse is covered by a pendentive cupola. The pensile monks' choir, with its five arches, runs the length of the church and creates a vestibule space which is quite distinct from the rest of the church. This monumental marble choir, given a myriad of decorations, uses architectural materials and forms that hark back to Lombardian models; it imposes its refined presence on a church that is otherwise enlivened only by the chromatic composition of the floor and discs along the walls. A Tuscan doorway leads to the Croce chapel, which was paid for by the Priuli family and which was most certainly not a part of the original project. The simplicity of the church was innovative for a Venice given over to exaggeratedly heavy-handed tastes; however, not only did Venetians come around to the idea quite quickly, but they then also assumed the church as a new model.

A much later addition is the hexagonal Emiliani chapel (1527), which was built just to the left of the prospect. The pointed portal, containing the Gothic *St Michael and the Dragon* sculpture, leads to the 15th century cloister and cemetery.

Torcello e Murano

This series of buildings, made up of a Baptistery, the Basilica of Santa Maria Assunta and the church of Santa Fosca, is one of the few examples left to remind us of Torcello's original splendour (in the 10th century Torcello had more than 10,000 inhabitants). The buildings seem to have been organised to symbolise the Christian conception of life: the baptistery symbolises birth; the basilica life itself; the church, containing the remains of the martyr, death leading to celestial life.

51 – The Baptistery

The original 7th century building was circular and had eight columns, just like Roman thermal baths. The ruins can still be seen in front of the basilica.

52 – Santa Maria Assunta
11th century

Founded in 639, according to the epigraphic inscription to the left of the choir, the church was reconstructed in 1008 by Orso Orseolo, son of Doge Pietro II, when he became bishop of Torcello. The Veneto-Byzantine plain stone building has three naves, a central, raised façade with six pilaster strips and a portico. The portico originally had four columns, to which a further series was added on either side and which linked the portico to the church, forming a unitary structure in the 14th and 15th centuries (the wooden beams were modified in the same period). The side of the church is dominated by the large square bell tower (12th century), demonstrating the economic and political kudos the island had acquired (Pomposa and Aquileia, for example, used the same emblem). Under Orseolo the church was extended, the apses rebuilt, the central apse area heightened and a crypt placed under the choir. The well-lit triple nave area, containing tall columns with Roman capitals (some of which are original, others Venetian imitations), recalls Ravenna's Sant'Apollinare Nuovo. The central nave, with its large arches, is separated from the side aisles by nine Greek marble columns with Corinthian capitals surmounted by a low pulvin.

The marble mosaic floor was raised 20 centimetres higher than the original 9th century floor, the black and white motifs of which can still be admired through two "viewing windows" placed in the floor. Different colours highlight different sections in the church: the central nave has prevalently grey geometric patterns; the side isles are predominantly red marble; the presbytery a series of multi-coloured "wedges" forming a circular design. The presbytery also contains a burial stone dedicated to Paolo di Altino, and houses the iconostasis with a sacred door at its centre, surrounded by three columns partly enclosed within 11th century Byzantine marble plutei covered by images of lions, flowers and peacocks drinking from a divine fountain. The columns support 15th century tables depicting the Madonna surrounded by the Apostles, which in turn supports a wooden crucifix from the same period. To the left, between the presbytery and the nave, there is a marble ambo made from fragments of the 7th century church. Some historians maintain that there were originally two ambos per side, reduced to one in the early 13th century - the lowest, held up by a small polygonal column, was used for readings from the Epistles, while the other, much more elaborate, ambo was used for the New Testament. The altar, with its Greek marble covering, was reconstructed in 1939 following original examples. At its feet, protected by a grate, there is a 3rd century Roman sarcophagus containing the body of St Heliodorus, bishop of Altino.

Just beyond the altar the huge, there is the conch-shaped apse containing the bishop's throne (the same structure was used for the 5th century Santa Maria delle Grazie, in Grado). The throne is placed on a round dais. The ten steps leading to the throne represent the ten commandments. During the 1939 restoration, Benedictine-style frescoes (subsequently covered by marble slabs, probably in the 12th century) were uncovered. Above the bishop's throne there is a mosaic representation of St Heliodorus. The Apostles, bearing their own specific symbols (as was common in the Ravenna churches), are symmetrically disposed at the feet of the Virgin Mary. At the centre of the procession there is a small window, symbol of the light of God, and a 12th century Byzantine Madonna, sumptuously dressed and isolated within the golden concave void, symbolising the marriage of the divine and the human. She is holding the

Child in her arms, and a white handkerchief, a symbol for the *Mater Dolorosa*, in her hands. Christ is holding a scroll, probably containing the Church laws.

The apse of the right side chapel, decorated in 864 and restructured in the 11th-12th centuries, contains representations of four church fathers - Ambrose, Augustine, Gregory and Martin. Above them is an enthroned Christ holding law tablets and surrounded by the Archangels Michael and Gabriel. The cross-vault is decorated with a series of angels holding aloft a large medallion containing a representation of the Mystical Lamb against a blue background. These are surrounded by floral and animal motifs, symbolic allusions to the Evangelists. The iconographic and stylistic technique are again reminiscent of the Ravenna style, especially that of San Vitale (6th century). The left side chapel contains fragments from a 13th century fresco. Jacopo Tintoretto's small altar-piece, The Virgin Mary, can be found in the same aisle. An enormous mosaic sequence, *The Last Judgement* (11th-12th centuries), occupies the entire west wall, and was designed to remind the faithful of their fate as they left the church. The mosaic is divided into six sections, and was meant to be "read" from top to bottom, that is from the Crucifixion to the scene in which the bad are being culled from the good. This final scene is a marvellous example of naturalistic representation, and is intense and radically Venetian (identical naturalistic narration can be found in St Mark's, where the same mosaicists later worked on the large narrative mosaic sequences).

The basilica still has a small window covered by an alabaster strip, used to give the church its own special light. On the external façade there is also a series of strange Istrian stone "shutters".

53 – Santa Fosca
11th century

The saint's body was brought to the island in the 10th century from Sabratha, a Punic city near Tripoli. In fact, the Santa Fosca cult is linked with medieval trade routes. The church was originally intended as a *martyrium* (that is, dedicated to a Church Martyr), and is a typical example of 11th century Byzantine church architecture (a square inscribed within an octagon). Three wings extend from the central area, and have barrel vault ceilings. The fourth wing contains the presbytery, with three apsed naves preceded by a double line of blind arches. The structure is very similar to that of San Donato on Murano. The cupola over the central square area of the building has a series of hexagonal "sails". The solemn simplicity of the interior is typical of the Byzantine conception of space.

The polygonal portico surrounding the church (extending along five of the eight external sides of the building) has raised Veneto-Byzantine arches. The same type of arch can be found in a few Venetian palazzi (Ca' Loredan and Ca' Farsetti, for example). Originally the eclectic columns and capitals contained a series of fixed marble plutei (only parts of which have survived). The building is an admirable example of geometrical equilibrium and harmony.

54 – Santi Maria e Donato
11th – 12th centuries

Founded in the 7th century by refugees from the mainland, the church was transformed and enlarged after the year 1000. According to the date inscribed on the main floor, the church was completed by 1140. The church was dedicated to St Donatus and St Mary in 1125, when St Donatus' body was brought back from Cephalon along with the dragon he had slain. The saint's body was buried in the basilica (now in the main altar), while the dragon was purportedly buried in the baptistery area.

The church is a masterful blend of the Eastern traditions of early Venetian buildings (Torcello, for example) and the constructive and plastic developments of Romanic architecture. During restoration work undertaken on the building by Camillo Boito between 1858 and 1873, the original brick church was brought to light. The enormous surfaces are lightened by a series of pilaster strips, blind arches and Veneto-Byzantine arched lintels. The unadorned main façade, facing a solitary campo, is typical of basilicas and points to the internal three-naved structure of the church. Fragments of Roman memorial stones with portraits (2nd century) were used to decorate the side counterforts. Above the doorway there is a 14th century bas-relief showing St Donatus with a devoted follower. A splendid hexagonal apse was built alongside the canal, one of the main transport routes of the island. The lower order of the apse has a fake portico of seven blind arches contained within a series of paired columns; the upper order has a corresponding "gallery" of Istrian stone columns and parapets. The two are linked by a series of Veneto-Byzantine marble motifs and fired brick friezes.

The isolated square bell tower (12th-13th centuries) has three orders of pilaster strips and a three-light mullioned window belfry.

The interior of the church has been organised according to rigorous geometrical rules demonstrating a highly sophisticated use of form and give the whole a sense of great harmony. The naves are separated by a double series of Greek marble columns, with refined Veneto-Byzantine capitals. The distance of the columns is mathematically proportional to the length of the side aisles. In turn, the side aisles, along with the transept and the

wing of the main apse, are proportionally related to the central nave. The early 15th century wooden ceiling has the uniquely Venetian "ship's keel" form. The splendid mosaic floor, which is very similar to that of St Mark's, was made using two different techniques: the so-called *opus sectile*, using only stones, and the *opus tessellatum*, using marble and polychrome glass tesserae.

Like Torcello, the concave surface of the central apse is decorated with a glowing, golden covering highlighting the Virgin Mary, perfectly in keeping with Byzantine canons. According to Barbaro, the Virgin Mary is "retiring and maternal, refined and shy, a perfect symbol for this church; she is surrounded by no-one – not by her Son, her Father or her Husband. Like all examples of love, this one is equally absolute: the unknown artist chose to devote the entire field to her." Giottoesque frescoes are used to decorate the area under the Virgin.

In the left side aisle there is the *Ancona di San Donato*, one of the oldest of Venetian painted altar-pieces (12th century), probably by Paolo Veneziano. The small figures of the various donors, depicted using the Paduan style of realism, are in contrast with the saint's "flat" representation, which is still very much in the Byzantine tradition.

A few layouts

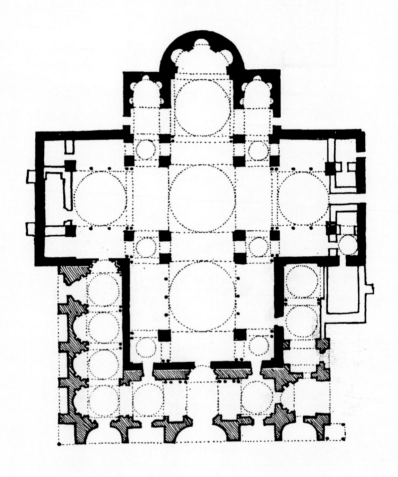

St Mark's Basilica,
Greek-cross layout

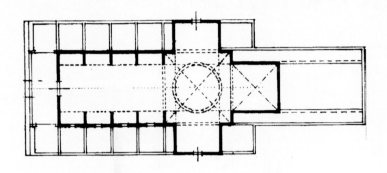

Church of San Francesco della Vigna,
Latin-cross layout

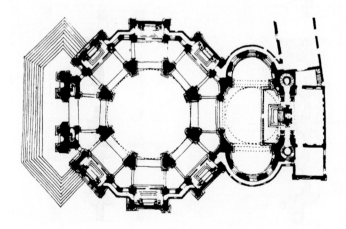

Basilica of Santa Maria della Salute,
Central layout

Select bibliography

AA.VV., *Storia dell'arte italiana*, Milan 1988.

ACKERMAN, J.S., *Palladio*, London 1974.

ARSLAN, E., *Venezia gotica*, Venice 1970.

BARBARO, P., *Venezia, l'anno del mare felice*, Bologna 1995.

BASSI, E., *Architettura del Sei e Settecento a Venezia*, Naples 1962.

BELLAVITIS, G.-ROMANELLI, G., *Venezia*, Rome-Bari 1985.

BETTINI, S., *Venezia, nascita di una città*, Milan 1978.

BRUSATIN, M., *Venezia nel Settecento. Stato, Architettura, Territorio*, Turin 1980.

CESSI, F., *Alessandro Vittoria scultore* (2 voll.), Trent 1982.

CONCINA, E., *Storia dell'architettura di Venezia*, Milan 1995.

ID., *Le chiese di Venezia. L'arte e la storia*, Udine 1995.

CORNER, F., *Notizie storiche delle chiese e monasteri di Venezia e di Torcello*, Padua 1758.

CUNACCIA, C.M.-SMITH, M.E., *Interni a Venezia*, Venice 1994.

D'ANNUNZIO, G., *Il Fuoco*, Milan 1995.

DAMERINI, G., *L'isola e il cenobio di San Giorgio Maggiore*, Florence 1969.

DORIGO, W., *Venezia: Origini, fondamenti, ipotesi, metodi*, Milan 1983.

FIOCCO, G., *Tiepolo*, Florence 1921.

FRANZOI, U.-DI STEFANO, D. *Le chiese di Venezia*, Venice 1976.

FRANZOI, U.-SMITH, M.E., *Canal Grande*, Venice 1993.

GEMIN, M., *La chiesa di Santa Maria della Salute e la cabala di Paolo Sarpi*, Abano Terme 1982.

GEMIN, M.-PEDROCCO, F., *Giambattista Tiepolo. I dipinti*, Venice 1993.

HEINEMANN, F., *Giovanni Bellini e i belliniani*, Vicenza 1962.

LORENZETTI, G., *Venezia e il suo estuario*, Triest 1974.

MCANDREW, J., *Venetian Architecture of the Early Reanaissance*, MIT 1980.

PALLUCCHINI, R., *La pittura veneziana del Trecento*, Venice-Rome 1964.

PALLUCCHINI, R.-ROSSI, P., *Tintoretto, le opere sacre e profane*, Milan 1982.

PIGNATTI, T., *L'arte veneziana*, Venice 1989.

ID., *Venezia. Guida ai dipinti nei luoghi d'origine*, Venice 1995.

RITTER, D., *Ottocento. Immagini di Venezia 1841-1920*, Venice 1994.

ROMANELLI, G., *Venezia Ottocento*, Rome 1977.

ROMANELLI, G.-SMITH, M.E., *Portrait of Venice*, New York 1996.

SEMENZATO, C., *La scultura veneta del '600 e '700*, Milan 1986.

TAFURI, M., *Venezia e il Rinascimento*, Turin 1985.

ZUCCONI, G., *Venice. An Architectural Guide*, Venice 1993.

also German Edition